Toward Holy Ground

Toward Holy Ground

*Spiritual Directions for
the Second Half of Life*

Margaret Guenther

COWLEY PUBLICATIONS
Cambridge ✦ Boston
Massachusetts

Published in the United States of America by Cowley Publications, a division of the Society of St. John the Evangelist. No portion of this book may be reproduced, stored in or introduced into a retrieval system, or transmitted, in any form or by any means—including photocopying—without the prior written permission of Cowley Publications, except in the case of brief quotations embodied in critical articles and reviews.

Library of Congress Cataloging in Publication Data:
Guenther, Margaret, 1930–
Toward holy ground: spiritual directions for the second half of life /
Margaret Guenther
        p.   cm.
Includes bibliographical references
ISBN 1-56101-114-2
1. Middle aged persons—Religious life. 2. Aged—Religious life.
3. Spiritual life—Christianity. 4. Guenther, Margaret, 1930– . I. Title.
BV4579.5.G84   1995
248.8'4—dc20   95-19074 CIP

Editor: Cynthia Shattuck
Copyeditor and Designer: Vicki Black
Cover design by Vicki Black.

Scripture references are taken from the *New Revised Standard Version* of the Bible.

This book is printed on recycled, acid-free paper and was produced in the United States of America.

Cowley Publications
28 Temple Place
Boston, Massachusetts 02111

For Margaret Adah, Minnie, and Anne—
the grandmothers

When you realize where you came from,
you naturally become tolerant,
disinterested, amused,
kindhearted as a grandmother,
dignified as a king.

— Tao te Ching —

Acknowledgments

I am grateful to the trustees of the General Theological Seminary and to my faculty colleagues for the gift of time that enabled me to write this book. Professor William Doubleday, friend and neighbor, was especially generous in his support.

I am also grateful to my editor, Cynthia Shattuck, who combines the gifts of skilled midwife and spirited Little League coach.

As always, I am sustained by my husband Jack and his faith in me.

Table of Contents

Chapter One

Holy Ground

T he water in my well in Jenkins Hollow is very cold, even on the hottest summer days. It has come from deep underground, through layers of old rock. It tastes of iron, sometimes of sulphur, and leaves rusty stains on bathroom fixtures. Mr. Sisk the plumber suggests a filter, but I resist. I have come to love the distinctive taste, unlike the bland, heavily treated water of any other place in my life.

I remember pumping water on childhood visits to the country. It was a mysterious process, and I was especially puzzled by the need to prime the pump. Why did moving the handle up and down bring water from the depths, and why did it help to return some water to its source? Now the pump is electric, which is a great convenience, but the old mystery seems to have vanished, and water gushing from the depths is taken for granted.

One of the great mysteries of wells is knowing where to dig. In the past, people relied on the gifts of a dowser to help them locate the place where water could be found. I didn't know the word "dowser" until adulthood, since the common expression in the rural midwest of my childhood was "water witch."

My Uncle Henry was a water witch. He was a shabby old farmer; in his bib overalls, Uncle Henry could have been the model for Grant Woods's painting, *American Gothic*. An un-self-conscious man of few words, he took his gift for granted; it was to be matter-of-factly given away, but never sold. With a forked branch—hickory or willow would do—he would walk slowly over the ground until an unseen force tugged at the branch, pulling it toward the earth. "Dig here," he'd say. "Here's where you'll find your well." Uncle Henry witched wells all over his corner of Missouri. I wish that I had known him better, that I had better appreciated his simplicity and generosity when I was a child. A few times, when I have been alone in Jenkins Hollow, I have cut myself a forked branch of willow and walked slowly over the yard, just to see if the family gift has come down to me. It hasn't.

But I am convinced that we all have the ability to become dowsers, water witches, especially in the second half of our lives. We can respond to the tug that tells us where the wells are, that tells us who can lead us to the places where the underground sources of refreshment and sustenance can be found. Perhaps another definition for spiritual direction is holy water witching.

Sometimes, even though I can't make the willow branches work for me, I can feel the spiritual tug toward the deep and holy source and say to myself, or to the person who has turned to me in trust, "Dig here. Here's where you'll find your well." But there are also times when I need help to find my own well; I sometimes feel as if I have drained the last drops from the waterskin and am surrounded by aridity. Then I need the help of a fellow dowser.

When we have discovered where to dig, plumbed the depths of the well, drunk from it, and embraced its coolness and its darkness, we will find ourselves on holy ground. Like the burning bush that cannot be extinguished, the well that cannot be used up is a picture of God.

The Second Half of Life

This book is about the questions that rise up to meet us in the second half of live. I approach them as a priest but also as a woman, a teacher (I was delighted one day last spring when a student called me "Rabbi"!), a wife, a mother, and a grandmother. And even should I not be blessed with the longevity and vigor of my maternal grandfather's family, I am well into the chronological second half of life. I was touched and amused a few years ago when a young colleague observed, "Margaret, you have a remarkably brisk walk for a middle-aged woman." I pointed out to him that, if I were really at midpoint, we could look forward to my living for another sixty years—unlikely and not especially desirable.

I am also writing as a spiritual director, even though this book is not an instructional manual, nor am I writing about the ministry of spiritual direction per se. I am more concerned with ways of *being* than ways of *doing.* My aim is twofold: first, to explore how we can minister, befriend, and accompany one another in the second half of life, and, second, how we can shape our lives and discern the unique insights, griefs, and opportunities of that part of life.

Despite my own chronological age and my work with and great love for the frail aged, however, this is not a "sunset years" book. The second half of life cannot be calculated by consulting the actuarial tables, for it is not really a matter of physical age. Particularly as we live with the plague of AIDS, it is an absurdity to equate the second half of life with attainment of a certain number of years.

Even those not directly affected by AIDS have an awareness of mortality undreamed of a few decades ago. Leah, a friend who lives in a predominantly gay and lesbian community, told me about her most recent loss: she had been called by a good friend who was keeping vigil when his young partner died of AIDS. Kevin couldn't be sure: maybe Tony wasn't dead, maybe it was all a mistake. He needed Leah to stand by him and tell him that life was really gone from the body he had loved. Leah told me how she touched Tony and listened in vain for his breathing, then wept with Kevin. "I couldn't have done that a few years ago, but I've got used to dead bodies. They don't scare me, but I'm getting sick of death. I've been to too many funerals. I've lost too many people. None of the men I knew when I moved here eight years ago is still alive. Even when we don't talk about it, we are all thinking about death, wondering who will be next." She knows about pain, loss, and transience, and she has seen the human body at its most degraded and tormented. Leah may live for another fifty years—she is barely thirty now—but she is already well into the second half of her life.

Leah's circumstances are dramatic and tragic. For many of us, however, awareness of arrival at life's turning point coincides with an increase of realism in our workaday lives. There is no drama, no soap opera—just the unavoidable perception of reality. This can be disappointing: we feel cheated that the prizes we sought are unattainable or that they turn out to be the tawdry merchandise offered by the carnival barker. It is not easy to give up delusions; and when we finally do so, we may feel liberated—or defeated.

Although he did not acknowledge it, my friend Harry was glimpsing his own mortality when he realized at fifty-five that he would advance no further up the corporate ladder. Despite a six-digit income and a prestigious title, dissatisfaction was gnawing at him. He was sure that there was something more and that it should be his. Our secular theology has no place for mortality or limitation: there must always be new frontiers to conquer. Of course, there is something more, but Harry cannot see it. Yet. He has built his life around his job. Not atypically for men (and increasingly, women) in our culture, his god has been the narrowly conceived god of success. I cannot predict what will happen: he may grow more tired and bitter, resigned to a barren existence, or he may see the present reality of his life as an invitation to new growth and vitality. He may rediscover passion. I would never use the language of conversion in a conversation with Harry, but he is ripe for the experience.

As a rule, we do not know precisely when we enter life's second half, although for some of us awareness of mortality comes suddenly and sharply. But when my young colleague commented on the briskness of my walk, I had to pause and think for a moment. I was feeling middle-aged at most that day, really kind of thirtyish. I had to do a little rapid arithmetic to convince myself and him that I was well along on the other side of the hill.

So what *is* the second half of life? It is when we are finally grown up (which is *not* the same as ceasing to grow). We have experienced the autonomy yearned for by teenagers: we revel in our many choices and our ability to control many details of our lives. But with that freedom, we also experience responsibility and, ultimately, our own limitation. We realize too, perhaps gradually and reluctantly, that our hard-won autonomy is fleeting if not illusory. Our bodies let us know in great ways and in small that we will not live forever. We know that we are not God. We know that we are mortal, even though it is possible to deny this knowledge for long periods of time.

The second half of life is also the age of the amateur. Amateurs are lovers, drawn to their work and their commitments by love, not duty, sustained by the gift of joy and wonder in all God's works. In the first half of life, our energy is devoted to proving ourselves, maybe even to discovering whether we have—more important, *are*—a self. This is the time for degrees and credentials, for developing a professional identity. This is the time for being in love. In the second half of life our perspective changes, and we are amazed to realize that some things just don't matter any more.

This change in perspective struck me when I entered seminary after nearly a half-century of proving myself. One of the first occasions of academic accountability was a map test in Old Testament. We were given blank maps and instructed to locate a number of significant places—twenty of them, or was it fifty? The number doesn't matter. I understood well the pedagogical impulse behind the test: it was important for us to know that we were reading about real people who lived in real places, that references to mountains and rivers and roads were not merely metaphorical. But there was something repellent about reducing the wonder of place, especially the place of encounter with the holy, to a quiz scored on the basis of 100. As I took my pen in hand and looked at the blank map, my hand began to shake and my mouth went dry. How would it look if the former professor flunked the map test?!

I can't remember my score, but it was good enough—not outstanding, but good enough. I do remember the resolve that flooded over me when I realized that grades and academic credentials—however valuable in practical terms—no longer mattered, for the tug toward God I was experiencing was not a career move. The identity I sought had nothing to do with degrees and titles. It went deeper, to a dark and unexplored place. And it wasn't about being in love, however delightful that condition might be. I was beginning to explore the difference between being in love and just plain loving. Even as I embarked on what outwardly looked like professional training, I was beginning to embrace my amateur status for the first time. I was ready to move from an arid landscape into a place of growth and new life, ready to turn and return to that holy place that Meister Eckhart called the origin and the ground.

The second half of life is a time of fruition, a spiritual fecundity which has nothing to do with human biology. The psalmist uses the imagery of trees planted in the house of the LORD: they are green and succulent when they might be expected to be brown and sere. The psalm speaks of palms and cedars, but I think of the tulip poplar of the Blue Ridge, green and succulent even in times of drought because its roots have sought and found water deep beneath the ground.

In the second half of life, we are able to embrace ambiguity. I am stunned when I realize how little I know and how every year I seem to know less and less. Perhaps this reflects the impoverishment of the English language; we have only one word for "know," whereas French, German, and Spanish are vastly more nuanced. In German I can know facts, hard data, things demonstrable, definable, and provable—*wissen*. I can know a language in a way that links its competent use with the intellectual grasp of it—*können*. So when I say, *"Ich kann Englisch,"* I am saying that I can understand, speak, write, and think in that language. I can use it. Further, I can know people, countries, books, and music—*kennen*. This can indicate a casual acquaintance, but at its best implies a deeper, richer kind of knowing, not easily measured and never static. Finally, there is the knowing that is almost a numinous experience—*erkennen*. This is the knowing of profound understanding, of the grasp of hidden connections. This is the knowing of insight and wisdom.

In the second half of life we begin to let go of the kind of knowing dedicated to the pursuit of the demonstrable, definable, and provable. The amassing of data becomes just one more form of acquisition. And we begin to take for granted the knowing that expresses itself in useful competence. To offer a homely example: after decades in the kitchen, I "know" cooking the way I know my native language. My hands know when bread dough has been kneaded sufficiently, and my ears know the "whistle" of a perfectly sauteed mushroom. Cookbooks have become recreational or possibly inspirational reading; but the real "knowing" of food preparation resides somewhere deep within me.

The knowing that characterizes the second half of life is open to mystery, drawn to the depths, and ready to risk. It is not easily distracted by minutiae. The questions it raises are rarely multiple choice or true-false. Embracing ambiguity leads to a kind of holy agnosticism, a comfortableness with mystery and open-endedness. It is the time we begin to ask ourselves: What do I really know? What matters? What is the rock-bottom of my faith?

In the old days, the millers in Jenkins Hollow ground grain between two great stones. The top one, the runner stone, moved with the force of the water. The bottom one, the bed stone, was solid, level, and unmoving. What we know, deeply know, in the second half of life is like that bed stone. It is what matters.

In Search of a Saint

In the second half of my life, I realized that I needed a saint. As an aging, mildly feminist, rather conventional Episcopal priest, wife, mother, and grandmother, I needed a saint. Sometimes the ineffable, unknowable God was (and is) simply too much for me. Theological tomes made my head swim. There were so many big words, such feats of inexorable logic, so many abstractions. God had to be both so much simpler and so much more profound than our attempts to capture him. Her. My prayer and my dreams lured me on to new places. My encounters with Christ's wounded body on the streets of a polyglot city and my glimpses of the awesome beauty of creation in the night sky of the Virginia Blue Ridge invited me: push out the boundaries, trust, let go.

It is ironic that I should feel in midlife, after decades of faithful attendance and devotion to the church, that tug toward God, that mysterious pull to go adventuring that has seemingly little to do with previous ecclesial faithfulness or observance. To respond to that invitation is to let the feet leave the floor, to let go of the railing around the rink—I'm not a skater—and to take off the training wheels. To give oneself over to the exploration is to embark on the journey described by W. H. Auden, "to see strange beasts and to have unique adventures."

It is easy to talk about letting go. Indeed, it has become part of our popular piety, thanks to the various Twelve Step programs, and we see the slogan on bumper stickers: "Let go, let God." The act of surrender, though, is something else. In the second half of life, it can feel like a lonely plunge. A departure from sensible everydayness. A second coming of age, just at the time society suggests we think about winding down. At a time like that, the company of a saint would be welcome.

But I also knew that not just any saint would do. Like the family album of our biological relations, the company of the saints contains a fair number of eccentrics, people who might have been hard to live with, people whom we might respect but don't want to get too close to. Just imagine some of these saints gathered with the family at the dinner table!

I think of Pambo, who lived in the fourth-century Egyptian desert. To divert attention from his natural good looks, he refused to wear anything but rags—the more tattered the better, and preferably so disgusting that no one else would even touch them. As a spiritual discipline he avoided speech, so his friends found him either silent or brusque to the point of rudeness.

Christina the Astonishing, a holy virgin of the Middle Ages, could not bear the smell of sinful human bodies so she climbed trees, crawled into ovens, and even flew up to roof beams of churches to escape them. She seemed impervious to fire and occasionally jumped into rivers. She's the kind of relative people whisper about, and they breathe a sigh of relief when she refuses the invitation to the family reunion.

St. Simeon of the sixth century began living on a pillar when he was seven—"before he had lost his first teeth," the legend tells us. (Where were his parents? They could have compared notes with Pambo's parents on the problems of child-rearing!) He lived on a pillar for fifty-five years and was ordained priest without coming down; a platform was built for the ordaining bishop, and disciples climbed a ladder to receive communion from him. He was indeed a holy man, but hardly mainstream.

In looking for a saint to keep me company at this time in my life, I found myself paying increasing attention to the women saints. They are nearly invisible in my place of daily worship, the seminary's Chapel of the Good Shepherd, where I am well into my second decade of fruitlessly scanning the windows and sculptures for supportive faces and figures. But not just any woman would do. For example, the virgin martyrs didn't attract me. I seem to remember a little street in Basel named for six thousand (or was it ten thousand?) virgins who marched blissfully to their terrible deaths. Even when I was much younger and a virgin, I had trouble seeing such folk as role models, guides, or friends. I was looking for strong women who somehow kept their feet on solid ground even as they trusted God's mysterious current to bear them up, strong women who managed to live to full maturity and die in their beds.

Dame Julian of Norwich was such a woman; she has accompanied me through a long part of the journey. She was wise, at home in her body and with all that is small and homely. She wrote of a God who loves maternally, who picks us up, dusts us off, and comforts us as if we were errant toddlers. Julian knew about suffering, but she did not let her knowledge of the depths and terrors overcome her. Similarly, Teresa of Avila, whose name is almost synonymous with mysticism, was very human, very much of the earth. The sculptor Bernini depicted her swooning in ecstasy, but her writings reveal a warmly practical woman who traveled through Spain in an ox cart, turned dirty and derelict buildings into convents, danced with her nuns, and approached even God with dryly affectionate humor. Both these sturdy women are as real to me as aunts or sisters.

But of course *the* woman saint, known to those who have never heard of Julian or Teresa, was Mary. Mary, Mother of God. Mary the God-Bearer, *Theotokos.* These words were simply not part of the mental or spiritual baggage of my midwestern Presbyterian childhood—nor, for that matter, of the comfortably broad church Anglicanism of most of my adult life. Mary belonged to the Roman Catholics. She was a suspicious—yet, for me, always attractive—figure. In my childhood I did not know the Mary of the Eastern icons, nor the Mary of Italian and Flemish paintings. The great mediatrix was mediated through humbler art forms: the Christmas card and that upended bathtub with a sky-blue interior. Occasionally she graced a bird bath.

As my own children were born and I knew the glorious and grubby realities of motherhood, I let myself grow closer to a different Mary, the earthly mother as I thought she might have been. Looking back on my own experience of motherhood, I wondered what we shared. Did she, like me, bestow a pet name on her unseen, unborn child? Did she ever tell him to clean up his room? Was he grounded upon return from the trip to Jerusalem? (By my standards of parenting, he should have been!) Did she sometimes raise her voice unfairly, scold or strike him in a burst of anger, or did she perhaps worry at his perfection and yearn for an ordinary, exasperating child? Did she wonder why he didn't bring home any nice girls? And, hard as it was, did she know when it was time to let him go, when her job was done? What was it like for her to watch him die?

I feel a sense of kinship with this human Mary, fruit perhaps of my imagination. Our shared experience of motherhood made me feel that I knew her, assured me she had much to give me. Yet even as I was drawn to this wise sister-figure, I could never forget her other, more awesome aspect: the God-

Bearer, the *Theotokos*. By turns melancholy, majestic, challenging, regal, triumphant, tragic, secretive, inviting, tender, and strong, always there was a sense that she possessed a deep inner knowledge, a knowledge of God's love and of the inevitable pain in human life. Even in her most stylized, remote depictions, she bridges the space between human and divine. More than a saint, she is the God-Bearer. One can love her, venerate her, rejoice at her inclusion in the theological inner circle. She is vastly reassuring, but she is not a cozy figure.

So I was still looking for my saint, but it was through Mary that I came to Anne. Perhaps it was a generational matter: as I myself grew older, I felt drawn to the idea of the *amma*, the *old* mother, to the concept of maternal love separated from procreation and physical birthgiving. Until then, I had never thought much about Anne. I knew only that churches bore her name, that there was an Episcopal women's monastic order of St. Anne, and that Martin Luther had reportedly cried out her name when he was struck down by lightning as a young man.

Suddenly I became aware of her as I saw more and more of her in sculpture and painting. I began to run across her in unexpected places, in pictures that I had looked at many times and in a familiar altarpiece in a favorite museum. She had been there all along, and I had paid her no attention. Then on a rainy January day, in a dark and cavernous gallery in what was formerly East Berlin, I stumbled on a magnificent, almost lifesize carving of *Anna Selbdritt*, and I knew I had found my patron and companion for the second half of my life.

Anna Selbdritt was a favorite subject of German artists of the late Middle Ages. The term translates badly: "Anne herself making three"—the mother, her virgin daughter, and the Christ child. There are minor variations, but Anne is always the dominant figure. Sometimes she is seated, regally enthroned, holding on her lap a small and girlish Mary, who in turn holds the Christ child. Sometimes, still majestic and imposing, she holds her daughter and her grandchild on either knee. Albrecht Dürer shows her as a plump and prosperous German matron, while Leonardo da Vinci has drawn a mysterious, ageless sibyl.

Just as I stumbled on the great carving of *Anna Selbdritt*, I came upon Leonardo's cartoon almost by accident. I knew that he began drawing a study of Anne holding her daughter, who is larger than she and who in turns hold the Christ child. But I had forgotten that it hung in London's National Gallery until last spring. I was avoiding the gallery altogether: I have done my time as a dutiful tourist, and now I resist the obligatory genuflection before great works. (This is one of the privileges of the second half of life!) When I am in foreign cities, I have come to prefer walking the streets or frequenting the stations, just to see ordinary people moving through their ordinary lives.

But on that particular day, something drew me to the National Gallery and I found myself in the small, chapel-like room where Leonardo's cartoon is displayed. The light is dim to protect the subtle browns, grays, and ochres of the drawing, and the room is small because no other work is displayed in it. In its darkness and smallness the space feels holy, no matter what the intentions of the curators. Unconsciously, I found myself reaching for a holy water font to bless myself as I entered. I sat for a long time before the crowded yet curiously serene drawing, trying to sort out the entanglement of legs and feet. Were those Mary's knees or Anne's? And was that Anne's hand—large, masculine, and barely sketched— pointing heavenward? Mary was young, pretty, the familiar Madonna. Anne was ageless, yet strangely young, with sharper features and an enigmatic smile.

This was no cozy German matron. This was indeed a sibyl: wise, knowing, and even a little bit sexy. No ordinary grandmother, by any means! I have found no other such depictions of Anne, but Leonardo's stands powerfully by itself and illuminates for me an aspect of her as a wisdom figure, someone who has lived long and seen everything and who is able to smile serenely at the totality of human experience.

The church and our culture are not particularly comfortable with the aging and the aged, and old women especially have a hard time of it. "Crone" is a bad word that needs to be reclaimed: the woman past childbearing years who is nevertheless still a woman, mysteriously maternal although far removed from birthgiving. God's grandmother, as limned by Leonardo, is such a figure. She is not merely an old, wise woman; she recalls the sibyls of legend, those mysterious figures of great antiquity. Originating in Asia Minor, they were adopted by Christian apologists as prophetic voices present from the earliest times. According to legend, a sibyl sailed on the ark with Noah.[1]

In other depictions of *Anna Selbdritt*, particularly those by German artists, Anne appears more like an earthly grandmother, caressing and playing with an earthly child held by an earthly mother. Typically, the Christ child looks to his grandmother rather than his mother, for she is the center of the group. The scene usually includes a book, sometimes held by Anne, sometimes by Mary; sometimes the child is reaching for it. I am still pondering the significance of this book. Some scholars explain it as a sign that Anne was responsible for her daughter's education and upbringing. Like all mothers, Anne was, of course, her child's first teacher: Mary learned to smile and to speak from her mother. A more compelling interpretation of the iconography is the explicit linking of Anne and Mary with Sophia, that fount of wisdom present at creation. Further, the inclusion of the book in this stylized family scene reminds us that Christ possesses the sum of all human knowledge.

---

1 For information about sibyls I am indebted to H. W. Parke, *Sibyls and Sybilline Prophecy in Classical Antiquity,* ed. Brian C. McGing (London: Routledge, 1988).

The extent to which Anne was venerated in the Middle Ages came as a surprise to me, as did the realization of what I had "always" known, namely that she is nonbiblical, completely legendary, and apocryphal. She is first mentioned in the *Protoevangelium of James* in the latter half of the second or early third century. Wife of a very rich man, Joachim, she bemoans her infertility; an angel appears and promises that she will bear a child. Anne pledges, "As the Lord my God lives, if I bear a child, whether male or female, I will bring it as a gift to the Lord my God, and it shall serve him all the days of its life." When the child is born, Anne asks the midwife, "What have I brought forth?" When she is told that she has borne a daughter, she says, "My soul is magnified this day."

The infant Mary takes seven steps at six months. Anne then vows that she shall walk no more until she is presented at the temple. The child is secluded—and presumably immobilized. When she is two years old, her father suggests that their promise be fulfilled, "lest the Lord send some evil upon us and our gift become unacceptable." Anne shows maternal tenderness: "Let us wait until the third year, that the child may then no more long after her father and mother." Set down on the third step of the altar, Mary danced for joy and never looked back.

The rest of the *Protoevangelium* is Mary's story; Anne does not reappear. But she came to occupy an ever-growing place in popular piety. Legends proliferated, as affection for "God's grandmother"—*Godz grotemoder*—grew. More than affection, there seemed to be a genuine *need* for Christ to have a grandmother and for his earthly family to be fleshed out. Anne was variously depicted as a wisdom figure, a mysteriously smiling sibyl, and a comfortably ample grandmother. Above all she was a matriarch, the center of a large and overwhelmingly feminine group of kin. Popular piety created "the Holy Kinship," which expanded Christ's family tree on the maternal side. According to legend, Anne married twice after Joachim's death and gave birth to two more daughters, also named Mary. They became the mothers of six of the disciples: James the Greater, Judas the son of James, Barnabas, Simon, James the Less, and John the Evangelist.

Pictorial representations of the fifteenth and sixteenth centuries show Anne as a loving grandmother, surrounded by her daughters and their children. It is a peaceful domestic scene: the wise and nurturing older woman, three young mothers, and a crowd of babies and toddlers tumbling on the grass. The women might be exchanging stories of childbirth or advice on child-rearing, not unlike their sisterly counterparts through the ages. They are sitting in an enclosed garden: the husbands and fathers are either relegated to the background, looking over the wall, or excluded completely. This is a world of mothers, not ordinary mothers by any means, but a remarkable sorority of closely related women divinely ordained to bear the Christ and his inner circle of followers.

The pictures could become large and complex, as relationships extended. As many as thirty people might be grouped around Anne or peering over the wall of the idyllic, idealized garden. The children sometimes carried symbolic objects, even instruments of their later martyrdom. For example, Simon often carries a saw and Judas a club. John the Evangelist is shown writing in a book, and James carries the pilgrim's shell. The whole scene is a parallel to the Jesse tree, emphasizing the maternal, earthly lineage of Christ. Indeed, a fifteenth-century hymn likens Anne to a tree:

Anne, the fruitful root,
   the health-bringing tree,
you who have brought forth a three-fold branch
   laden with seven fruits.[2]

---

2 P. Beda Kleinschmidt, OFM, *Die heilige Anna: Ihre Verehrung in Geschichte, Kunst und Volkstum* (Duesseldorf: Schwann, 1930), p. 272. My translation.

The scene in the enclosed garden cuts through theological abstraction and offers the possibility of not one but two Trinities. Typically, God the Father is in the sky, watching over the scene in the garden, while the Holy Spirit descends as a dove directly over the Christ child. The matriarchal, earthly trinity is, of course, comprised of Anne and Mary, with the child between them. It is an immensely satisfying picture of the union of divine and human.

At the heart of it sits the grandmother in the garden. If she is a typical grandmother, she is convinced that the child she holds is perfect, gifted, and beautiful. She has no trouble loving him unconditionally and his divinity is easily apparent to her, for grandmothers can see the divinity in every child even when the parents cannot.

There are no Annes in the hagiography of our popular culture. Her brand of wisdom is not at home in the pages of popular magazines nor in the Pentagon—nor even in the church, Mother Teresa notwithstanding. It is time for us to rediscover and reclaim St. Anne, to recognize the truth, love, and ambiguity she personifies even as we accept her legendary status. The Anne of legend is strong and reliable, a source of wisdom born of long experience and closeness to ordinary human life. Perhaps what Anne represents has been rendered invisible and neglected, not just by the church but by the whole culture, because her beauty and (more important) her power are feared. To accept what Anne offers might call for letting go of old fears. It might call for new openness and willingness to change.

St. Anne stands as patron to my reflection and conversation about the spirituality of the second half of life. Like many grandmothers, she fits comfortably into the background; like most, she's been around and has much wisdom to offer, wisdom about ways of living and working together and about ways of dying. The chapters that follow reflect pieces of her story and bits of her symbolism. Throughout the centuries,

Anne has been identified not only with the holy family of Jesus, with its emphasis on kinship and connection, but also with fruitfulness, healing, artistry and craft, birth, and the blessing of a "good death." She can give us the companionship we need as we navigate the second half of life in all its richness and ambiguity. As a member of Jesus' family tree, she reminds us of the need for kinship and connection at this time of life. As the patron saint of guilds and artisans, she helps us focus on the necessity of discipline and rule, the essentials of crafting a life and the discernment of new "spiritual directions."

Finally, St. Anne is the patron saint of the harvest, of healing, wholeness, and fruition, and for centuries men and women prayed to her as one who could bestow a good and holy death. She can go before us as we approach holy ground, where we will find ourselves at the place where we started and will know it for the first time.

— Chapter Two —

Kinship

I n the legends of Anne, late medieval popular piety surrounded the infant Jesus with an extended family—aunts,
uncles, cousins, and, of course, a grandmother. Despite
his rejection of traditional familial claims—"Who are my
mother and my brothers?"—legend supplied Jesus with
scores of relatives and worked out intricate patterns of kinship. On the paternal side, God the Father sufficed. But the
maternal side of the family tree was crowded. After all, to be
truly incarnate Jesus needed human kin.

This seems to be the point of the Holy Kinship pictures and
elaborate genealogical tables detailing Anne's other children
and grandchildren. Just as late medieval art emphasized the
human suffering of the crucified Jesus and as devotion to the
creche underscored his infant vulnerability, depictions of the
Holy Kinship made clear that God did not take on human
flesh in isolation. To be incarnate was to be part of a family.
Popular piety supplied what Scripture neglected to mention!

It is easy to take the message of the Holy Kinship one step
further: just as the Christ child was born not merely to a human mother but into a human family, *the* human family, so
we too are part of the Holy Kinship. Even the most misan-
thropic and introverted among us is part of that intricate web
of connection. Like it or not, we are *all* related. So in the sec-

ond half of life we need to explore ways of being together that honor the holiness in our human kinship. It cannot be said too often that Christian spirituality, of whatever time of life, is a spirituality of relationship. With its changed perspective, the second half of life—whenever it comes to us chronologically—invites reflection on the meaning of "family."

In our culture, however, the crowded garden of the Holy Kinship pictures exists chiefly in television commercials for cameras, lemonade mix, and greeting cards. The effectiveness of these advertisements carries a powerful truth: we are yearning for kinship, and we are homesick for home, the warm and untidy home of extended and often tangled relationships. I am struck by the number of such advertisements that feature very old people, grandparent figures placed at the center of the family reunion. They unite the family simply by their being. Perhaps I have come to see Anne everywhere, or perhaps she has indeed invaded Madison Avenue and is sending us subliminal messages.

From the perspective of life's second half, Jesus' seemingly harsh treatment of his mother and brothers is not so much a rejection of his biological family as it is a command to enlarge that family. When he says, "Here are my mother and my brothers! Whoever does the will of God is my brother, and sister, and mother," he is inviting us to enlarge the garden. We can smile at the naiveté of the Holy Kinship stories that turn disciples into first cousins and supply Jesus with two aunts bearing the same name as his mother. (They are reminiscent, by the way, of the confusing cluster of Marys in the resurrection stories.) But the truth remains: we are all related—not just to the people in our lives, in the here and now, but to people very unlike us whom we shall never meet in the flesh but in the mystical communion of all the saints, past, present, and to come.

I do not regret the gradual breaking down of my small garden walls as my children grew up, or at least their reconfiguration and expansion. In the second half of life, our view of family and kinship can broaden—indeed must broaden—if we are to keep alive and to grow spiritually. The process can be poignant, sometimes painful; it is easy to see only the losses, and not the inviting open doors. For a long time now, I have not been anyone's child—although sometimes I want to be. I try to remember my parents' voices and find that after the passage of decades I cannot recall them. (Did my father retain a German accent from his childhood? What did my mother sound like when she spoke to me as an infant?) Yet at the same time I am drawn close to the German grandparents whom I never knew, the dour great-grandfather who left Scotland in 1837 (why?), the invalid great-grandmother Hannah who died when her children were babies, and a whole series of frontier foremothers who bore children, toiled in their gardens, and left no words for me. It is an easy move—*ein Katzensprung*, a cat jump—from this circle of immigrant and pioneer kinship into one that is unimaginably larger.

In recent years the gay and lesbian community has given us a model of holy kinship in its response to AIDS. People who may never have heard the biblical question, "Who are my mother and my brothers?" have demonstrated that they know the answer in their faithful care of the sick. In the tradition of Francis of Assisi, who urged his friars to "mother" one another, they have become dedicated caregivers.

I witnessed this when Jim, a gay friend, spent a few days in my house. He had asked if he might bring a buddy who had always wanted to visit New York. When they arrived, I realized that Ron was very sick with AIDS, scarcely able to travel. I was puzzled by their relationship: I knew that Jim had been alone for years and wondered why or how he would commit himself to a partner in such poor health. Then he told me the story. He had known Ron for only a few months. Ron was still grieving the death of his partner of fifteen years even as he faced his own lonely death. His Fundamentalist parents had banished him from their home and predicted his damnation.

"So I decided to move in with him," Jim told me. "He doesn't have long. He's burning up inside, and he keeps having these little strokes. They're getting worse, and one of them will probably take him out. He's a sweet guy, and nobody should have to die alone; he needs somebody to be with him while he waits it out."

For the next few days I watched Jim be mother and brother to Ron, risking loss of his job to create comfortable time and space around his sick friend. "It doesn't really matter," he said when I asked him about his own career. "I can always get a job, and I'll just start over after Ron is gone."

Jim and Ron are icons for me of what Christ's extended family can be. But it is important to remember that holy kinship can be joyous as well as painful, filled with rewards as well as sacrifice. Now that my nest is empty, I am free to discover new ways of mothering that have little to do with the absorbing work of biological motherhood. I am able to be with people younger than I, to resist the temptation to mold them in my image, and to rejoice that I am privileged to witness and support their growth. Whether they are seminarians, directees, or simply friends, I can love them, care for them—and let them go.

The Call to Community

Part of the work of the second half of life is the seeking out of community in a broader vision of kinship. This vision does not come to us automatically, but disappointment is inevitable if we stand outside, calling for Jesus to come out, when our place is with the crowd that is sitting about him. I do not suggest that those in the second half of life have a special claim on community, but those who have accepted their own mortality have an easier time of letting go of impediments that keep them standing outside the door. They can move more easily into the crowd, that crowd around Jesus. They are our kin, our community.

So what is this community we are drawn to in the second half of life, and how do we find it? First and most obviously, there is our relationship to one another in a eucharistic, worshiping community. This seems self-evident, but I encounter a disturbing number of isolated seekers. Honest and intense in their search, they come seeking a referral to a spiritual director. Spiritual direction undertaken as a private path to mystical experience is a mischievous, even perilous enterprise—and it isn't spiritual direction. Early in the interview I always ask: "Tell me about your faith community." If there is none, I suggest that finding a congenial, welcoming parish is the first step. It may require long and patient searching, but there is a sense of homecoming when the seeker finally walks through the door and knows, "This is it." Despite my bias in favor of the Episcopal Church, I urge the potential directee to "shop around," visit freely, breathe the air, and test the waters. I encourage lapsed Roman Catholics to try going home again.

Sometimes the community we are searching for is not where we expect it to be. Elise, for example, was brought up in a nonobservant Jewish home and attracted to Anglicanism for romantic and aesthetic reasons, drawn mainly from novels and movies. Though she came to me for spiritual direction, I had no sense of conversion in her; she seemed drawn to externals rather than to Christ, at least at that point in her life. While I assured her that the ubiquitous signs on the street corners were indeed sincere and that the Episcopal Church *did* welcome her, I counselled that she should explore her own rich heritage. I couldn't be her spiritual director because we did not share the essential premises. I could, however, remain her friend, talk with her from time to time, and keep her in my prayers. If she remained open and seeking, I was convinced that she would find her community.

It is easier to theorize about community than it is to build it, live in it, and embody it. As a member of the seminary admissions committee, I interview many prospective students and have learned to be attentive to their expectations of our life together. Our enclosed block of quaint brick buildings clustered around the imposing Victorian Gothic chapel and beautifully tended gardens (a New York version of Anne's *hortus conclusus)* promises a kind of quasi-monastic coziness. Almost as a reflex, I try to dampen the candidate's enthusiasm as I point out the difficulties of diverse people living, working, eating, praying, and studying in close proximity. Community doesn't simply happen, even in the most propitious physical setting, and loving intention is not enough. We know this from our experience as parents, children, sisters and brothers: no one escapes without wounds and scars. It takes real work to be part of an even moderately holy kinship.

Whether through physical limitations or through choice, many of us make do with false community—the television set. Electronic warmth is more easily controlled than human warmth and can be measured out in desired doses; it can also be turned off and forgotten. The enormous popularity of television soaps has to reflect the paucity of meaningful relationships in the viewers' lives. The characters on the screen become more real—and more interesting—to their followers than their own lives. Similarly, television interview programs probing the most intimate and bizarre aspects of human relationships suggest that "real life" has become sterile, that it is better to be an emotional voyeur.

In the twelfth chapter of his first letter to the Corinthians, Paul reminds us of our interconnection:

> For just as the body is one and has many members, and all the members of the body, though many, are one body, so it is with Christ. (1 Corinthians 12:12)

The passage suffers perhaps from over-familiarity; we let the words slide over us without reflection:

> If the foot would say, "Because I am not a hand, I do not belong to the body," that would not make it any less a part of the body. And if the ear would say, "Because I am not an eye, I do not belong to the body," that would not make it any less a part of the body. (1 Corinthians 12:15-16)

Paul then goes on through the catalog of body parts. I recall myself as a child in church, seeing the possibilities of ribald humor if the list of examples were pushed to the limit, and wondering how our dignified and somewhat disembodied Dr. Matheson would manage from the pulpit.

Paul's words came back to me powerfully a few years ago when I slipped on the ice and sprained my right wrist. "No big deal," I thought, as the initial pain subsided. "It will be a nuisance for a while, but I still have another wrist, plus strong feet and legs and a relatively well-functioning brain. My wrist is only three percent of me"—a number pulled from the air—"so the other ninety-seven will get on just fine." Reality set in when I tried to dress the next morning! One hand working alone is a pitiful thing. Even walking on the snowy sidewalk was more difficult, for my minor injury distorted my balance and diminished my confidence. A wrist, I decided, is a humble thing, but it is part of the body. It is certainly no good apart from the body, and without it, the whole body suffers.

Spiritual Friendship

Spiritual friendship is a natural, integral aspect of kinship. Just as we, as Christians, must live within a community, often of diverse and not always compatible brothers and sisters, so also we must let ourselves be nourished and sustained by the more intimate relationship of friendship. Paul, with his perhaps undeserved reputation of being difficult to get along with, is again our guide:

> Speaking the truth in love, we must grow up in every way into him who is the head, into Christ, from whom the whole body, joined and knit together by every ligament with which it is equipped, as each part is working properly, promotes the body's growth in building itself up in love. (Ephesians 4:15-16)

This is the language of maturity and maturation: we grow up into Christ. This is the task of both halves of life, but one that we typically approach with a stronger sense of purpose in the second.

The term "spiritual friendship" may strike our ears as archaic, yet I know no better words to express this special, loving relationship. Whether we call them spiritual friends or soul friends, we need them desperately. Our relationships with them require intentional care and nurture. They are those people with whom we speak easily of Christ, whose prayers we ask, and whose discretion we trust. They may be theologically sophisticated, or they may be completely unlettered. We trust them because we recognize them as fellow travelers who are also growing up into Christ, fellow travelers who will speak the truth to us in love.

In the twelfth century, Aelred of Rievaulx describes such a friend:

> But what happiness, what security, what joy to have someone to whom you dare to speak on terms of equality as to another self; one to whom you need have no fear to confess your failings; one to whom you can unblushingly make known what progress you have made in the spiritual life; one to whom you can entrust all the secrets of your heart and before whom you can place all your plans![1]

---

1   Aelred of Rievaulx, *Spiritual Friendship* (Kalamazoo: Cistercian Publications, 1974), p. 72.

In many ways, this sounds like a skilled spiritual director, but at least some of these qualities can be found in our "ordinary" friends and colleagues as well. With them, we can let down our defenses and show our less-than-perfect selves. We can let go of the need always to be right. We can also "unblushingly make known what progress" we have made in the spiritual life. This is a great gift of spiritual friendship, for most of us find it inordinately difficult to acknowledge our own goodness and name our gifts. (This is not the same as insecure boasting or manipulative self-inflation for our own advantage.) Our spiritual friends can help restore our skewed perspective as they provide a much-needed reality check. They encourage us, give us heart. They are our mirrors and our midwives.

Finally, a spiritual friend is one to whom we can entrust all the secrets of our heart and before whom we can place all our plans. In other words, a spiritual friend offers a safe place to try things out, to stretch and to grow: we need not fear shaming or ridicule, no matter what we might say. I didn't know about Aelred, but I grasped this instinctively when I was a teacher of the German language. Some students came to the class convinced that their every utterance was either "right" or "wrong," and that they would be judged accordingly. The object of our work together then became the avoidance of "mistakes," which, when coupled with our innate fear of appearing "silly" or "dumb," brought all creative work to a halt. Such students were paralyzed, stuck at an immature and arid place. One anxious young man repeatedly submitted terse little compositions about the weather to fulfill an ongoing journaling assignment designed to foster freedom of expression. When I told him it was time to move on to more challenging topics—or perhaps to delve deeper into meteorology—he asked plaintively, "But what I'm writing isn't *wrong*, is it?" If he had seen me as a spiritual friend instead of a frightening teacher, he would have felt safe to try new things, to push out the boundaries, and to use his imagination, trusting in my undemanding, distanced love for him. He would have learned a new language.

The tradition of the *anamchara*—the soul friend—was well established when Christianity arrived in Ireland and Scotland, and so was easily incorporated into Celtic spirituality. The *anamchara* was a person of wisdom and integrity; in the early days a soul friend might be a woman or a man, lay or ordained, before the work of spiritual guidance became the prerogative of the clergy. Anyone might have a soul friend—St. Brigit among others is reported to have said that a person without a soul friend was like a body without a head—but particularly those in positions of power knew the need to enter into this relationship. The *anamchara* had the right to refuse the invitation: St. Patrick is reported to have turned away kings and chieftains. However, once the covenant was formed, the soul friend expected obedience and candor from the one who sought him out.

The world would be changed if, like the ancient Celtic chieftains, we all had spiritual friends, people who could speak the truth to us in love. We would hear words of comfort and words of challenge, occasionally words of reproach and concern. We would surely get angry sometimes, and at some point we would be forced to laugh (or at least chuckle) at ourselves. I fear that spiritual friends are rare in the corridors of political and economic power. Does the President have a spiritual friend, I wonder? Has the CEO of Citibank or Phillip Morris ever considered its usefulness? What would television be like if every network executive had a friend who spoke the truth in love?

Spiritual friendship demands candor, but it is always truth spoken in love. My heart sinks when a friend takes me aside and says in a confidential tone, "There's something I think you need to know." Maybe I do need to know it, but my defenses are already up and I am planning my denials. Figuratively, if not literally, my hands are clamped over my ears; and I can't help wondering if my friend is enjoying his moment over power over me. A painful variant is, "I'm telling you this for your own good," with the implied expectation of thanks for pain inflicted. This always reminds me of our pediatrician's nurse, who had the responsibility of giving injections. (The pediatrician wanted his small patients to think well of him, so they never saw him with needle in hand.) Just before the painful jab, she would say soothingly, "Mrs. Grimaldi loves you, John." Even by age two, John had figured out that this love was not mutual and that Mrs. Grimaldi did not share his pain.

Trust is the foundation of spiritual friendship, and guardianship of the tongue is a primary duty. Spiritual friends do not talk idly about one another, nor do they talk idly about others. Truth spoken in love is not the same as gossip in the name of truth. Gossip seems to me a typically "Christian" sin, for we can mask it as a sharing of loving concern: "I haven't told anyone else, but I know I can trust you" are dangerous words. Spiritual friends will inevitably carry burdens; they may know more than they want to know of another's hurts, shame, and fears. These are burdens they must carry alone, never forgetting that they can be lightened, even removed by giving them over to God in prayer.

How do we find these friends? Spiritual direction can sometimes turn into spiritual friendship, particularly after a long period of fruitful working together. Bit by bit, the conversations become more mutual, the director reveals more of herself, and the relationship changes. Shared work is another avenue to spiritual friendship, particularly when the work is demanding and meaningful. It may be the work of paid employment: the person at the next desk or in the next classroom is a potential spiritual friend. Or it may be work passionately cared about but unpaid. Thus we might find friendship in a shelter or feeding program, in some kind of shared effort that translates faith into action. Introverts, particularly, who might be reticent in spiritual formation and prayer groups, are more likely to reveal their deeper selves when engaged in actual *work*.

Spiritual friends also find one another in times of difficulty and crisis. Then there is little time or energy for banalities: rather, there is a kind of instant recognition and unspoken acknowledgment of spiritual kinship. This happened to me some years ago when I was on night duty as a chaplain in a large New York teaching hospital. I was called to the emergency room, where a woman was dying and her daughter, a Roman Catholic sister, had asked for a chaplain. She had been told that the chaplain on duty was Episcopalian, but she had not been told that it would be a woman. She embraced me as I entered the room and said, "I had been hoping I would meet a woman priest someday." Somehow I felt as if I had known her for a long time and that I didn't really need to explain anything about myself. I anointed her mother, who was then rushed off to surgery. Sister Rose and I sat down to wait in a dreary little room with orange plastic chairs, old newspapers, and discarded candy bar wrappers. As the night went on, we were joined by other members of her community. We didn't pray with words, but we sat in prayerful silence until dawn.

I have lost track of Rose now, but we stayed in touch for several years. In my office is a cross made of wheat that she gave to me as a token of our friendship. It is beginning to look a bit seedy, but I am afraid to take it down to dust it, so I will leave it there until it crumbles. I think of her from time to time, which I interpret as a sign to remember her in my prayers that night.

It would be comforting to think that the possibility of friendship always increases with the years and that old age always brings opportunities for true companionship, but reality suggests otherwise. One of the inevitable sorrows of living to an advanced age is the diminished circle: friends, colleagues, and siblings die so that the shared past is lost. Limited mobility narrows the circle further. During my years of nursing home chaplaincy, I saw few true friendships among the residents, in part perhaps because roommates were assigned as space became available. Consequently, there was often great disparity in almost every aspect of capability and interest: the alert and communicative might share a room with the near vegetative, the former professor with the former domestic, the Spanish-speaker with the man who had reverted almost entirely to Yiddish.

To be sure, there were exceptions. I always enjoyed dropping in on Bob and Al, who seemed genuinely to *like* one another. They exchanged stories—and mild complaints—about their busy children, admired pictures of grandchildren, and flirted with the younger nurses. Sometimes it seemed to me as if, for the first time since adolescence, they had the leisure for an easygoing friendship. On the other hand, Bertha and Edna, their neighbors across the hall, could hardly be called friends. They were both nurses, trained in the old school and proud of their profession, but instead of a sense of connection, which the home's staff had expected, they kept their juices flowing by an escalating and energetic rivalry. Whenever I encountered either in the elevator or the dayroom, I knew that I would hear the latest account of the other's transgressions. Somehow though, I suspected that they relied on each other and that their relationship was a very odd kind of friendship.

After spending a year as compassionate and companionable observer of life in a Massachusetts nursing home, Tracy Kidder has given a poignant and believable picture of friendship among the frail elderly. The protagonists of *Old Friends* are Lou and Joe, two very old men who differ in almost every way: Lou is an observant Jew, Joe a Catholic; Lou was a craftsman, Joe has a law degree; Lou can barely see, Joe can barely walk. In the forced intimacy of their circumstances, physical and spiritual, they have allowed themselves to become open and honest, supporting one another in ways impossible for family and staff to imagine. Their present is tenuous, and their future is death; the very limitation of material for conversation knits them together. As they lie on their beds in the evening and chat, their past becomes shared and their friendship makes them kin. The very repetitiveness of their lives, which the active young often find irritating, became a source of strength and comfort:

> The first times he heard Lou repeating himself, nearly a year ago now, Joe had decided to say nothing about it because Lou seemed like a nice guy, and he was old, really old. Joe felt differently now. He liked to hear Lou repeat his stories. He actually liked to hear them again. There was something beautiful about Lou in the act of storytelling, opening up his storehouse of memories and bringing them back to life.[2]

Intercession

As God's grandmother, seated at the center of the circle of Holy Kinship, Anne was invoked in the Middle Ages as a powerful intercessor. Young girls prayed for her help in finding a husband—after all, she had had three! Pregnant women relied on her for safe delivery; she knew about birth from experience, and by her own birthings had changed the world. Sailors, miners, and housewives turned to her to intercede on their behalf.

Intercession may become a distinctive vocation for many of us in the second half of life. The intercessor is a special kind of spiritual friend, for intercession is one way of living out the great web of kinship. Prayers of intercession come naturally, certainly more easily than prayers of confession and thanksgiving. Indeed, they may be our most common form of soli-

---

2   Tracy Kidder, *Old Friends* (New York: Houghton Mifflin, 1993), p. 183.

tary prayer, especially since we have often been socialized to think it "selfish" to pray for ourselves. Our earliest intercessions may have been appended to rote bedtime prayers; I remember concluding "Now I lay me down to sleep" with a list of those upon whom I asked God's blessing. It was a challenge to spin out the list as long as possible, and many of the people I prayed for were virtually unknown to me. I had never seen Great-Aunt Ellen, for example, but family piety dictated that she be included. Today I cherish Great-Aunt Ellen's gold thimble and enjoy the thought that my middle right finger somehow touches hers when I sew. She was a tough old lady who enjoyed baseball—the Cincinnati Reds were her team—and who in her eighties liked to read to elderly shut-ins. As a midwestern Presbyterian, she probably never heard of St. Anne, but I think they had a lot in common.

With our growing awareness of the web of connection, intercession becomes more powerful in the second half of life. We find that the present contains the past within itself and—if we are brave—the future as well. So there is a breathtaking simultaneity in our prayer: I can remember Anne Frank in her suffering, and I can look forward to pray for my unborn great-grandchildren. This simultaneity of intercessory prayer, its liberation from the strictures of time and place, can make it a costly kind of prayer. My childhood prayers for Great-Aunt Ellen were easy and cheap, for they were prayers of innocence. Innocence is not merely a state of being not guilty; it is also a state of ignorance and inexperience. In the second half of life, we are no longer innocents. We are shopworn, scarred, and bruised. Even the most sheltered among us has endured pain and glimpsed evil. Our prayers of intercession must reflect this hard-won and deeply ingrained knowledge. We must let ourselves be open to the suffering of those for whom we pray, must enter into it and let it enter into us.

Those for whom we intercede may be distant from us in time and place, personally unknown to us, yet this is an intimate form of prayer. As in spiritual friendship, three persons are involved: as we hold another before God, we are praying *through* Christ. And though it is intimate and may be in solitude, intercession (like any other prayer) can never be private, for we are praying in the community of the faithful. We are united in our sinfulness and in our glory as people created in God's image. Intercession is the prayer of our kinship.

To intercede means "to remain between, among, in the midst." So there is nothing remote or detached about intercession; we have to be *there*, between, among, and in the midst. We have to be willing just to stand there, before God, with the person being prayed for. I learned a great deal about this prayer of steadfast support from my friend Norah, a cancer survivor, when she told me the story of her surgery: "I was scared, really scared to death. Then I remembered—no, more than remembered—I could *feel* all the people who were praying for me. My family, of course, except I think they were too scared to do much praying. But all the people in my parish, some of my women friends who never go to church and probably wouldn't even call themselves Christian. They got me through that time, and that feeling didn't go away. The sense of all those people standing there with me—not literally, of course—stayed with me through chemotherapy and radiation and all the other hard times."

Simply to stand still before God on behalf of another is ultimately a passive stance, even though Scripture shows us that action and energy are also called for. This is a prayer of trust, of enormous faithfulness, of simply "hanging in." I don't know what intercessory prayer does, or how it does it—but it *does*. It is wrong to talk of success or failure, of results, even (in a way) of prayer answered. Sometimes the answer is silence.

I received a powerful lesson about intercession twenty years ago when a much-loved child in our parish was fighting leukemia. That parish was a web of connectedness, an earthly example of holy kinship, so many of us were involved in Kitty's struggle. She, her parents, and her brothers were constantly in our prayers. There were formal, spoken prayers, vigils, and—probably most important of all—a continuous and almost unconscious holding of her name before God. Just a few days before she died, her father said to me, "You know, even if we lose her, all this prayer has *worked.*" He couldn't tell me how, and somehow I was reluctant to ask. But I think I know what he meant: not just that troubled family, but the whole parish had been brushed by the Holy Spirit. The parents' grief was nearly unbearable, for who can endure the loss of a child? Both mother and father were perceptibly aged; they moved within a few months from being youthful to looking worn. Yet, at the same time, they were not defeated, and they never felt alone. They were able to see Kitty's short life as a gift and to feel God's presence even when their pain was greatest.

Some Practical Points about Intercession

It is enough simply to name the persons for whom we pray. There is always the danger of becoming prescriptive if we fill God in on their history and our perception of their needs. It is tempting to suggest to God that the single need mates, the childless need children, and the addicted need to find a Twelve Step program. Such intercession is rather like shopping: we come with our list and briskly check off items. Yet we can never really know the people for whom we intercede. Perhaps they are suffering from distress which no one suspects; perhaps there are deeper wounds hidden beneath the very obvious ones. Perhaps we have no sense of their need at all: we simply feel the urge to hold them for a moment before God. There is no hurry; just sit with a name and a face in silence, then a brief response—possibly "Lord, have mercy" or *"Kyrie eleison"* before naming the next person. For the strongly tactile, it might be helpful to pray intercessions with a rosary or other prayer beads. Then we are literally "holding" the person in our hand as we name her before God.

It may be helpful to keep a list of those for whom we pray. This is fine, so long as the method does not overshadow its purpose. In my language-teaching days, I always had students who liked to learn new vocabulary by making long lists and then trying to memorize them. It never failed: the first five words would be etched in their minds, then dimness would set in. Lists can lock us in, deprive us of spontaneity, and turn our intercessions into a chore. Yet used flexibly and weeded periodically, they can provide a supporting structure for our prayer.

Most of us begin by praying for those people closest to us—our families and other loved ones, our spiritual friends, and those dependent on us. Whenever I invite intercessions from retreat groups, I am reminded of this: people quite naturally name those closest to them. There is nothing wrong with this; in fact, it is very right. But it is easy to get stuck within this intimate circle. With maturity, our horizons should broaden from the narrow circle of those known to us to include all those in need or suffering, whole nations as well as individuals. When I quiet my words and let myself simply be open, I find myself praying for the people who are dying *right now*, the babies who are being born *right now*, the frail old woman lying sleepless in a nursing home *right now*, the prisoners who are being tortured *right now*.

Praying intercessions by categories keeps us from staying too close to home, or, more aptly, it reminds us that home is a big place and the family is large. We can pray for all prisoners, including prisoners of addiction and violence, and political prisoners; we can pray by name for those in positions of power. We can pray for the frightened and the despairing, the sick, the aged, all neglected and abused children, and all those who suffer.

It helps to have "icons" when we are praying for whole groups of people. For many months until his death, my young friend Lewis stood for all people dying of AIDS. When I remembered him as an individual, I also remembered all those whom I will never know but who share his suffering. Frankie, the homeless man who has been part of my life for the past three years, provides a face for all homeless people. An African American in his mid-thirties, he does not yet have the ravaged look that comes from years on the street; but when he has been drinking or when despair threatens to close in, I can glimpse the physical ruin that awaits him. Now, though, he is handsome, and on good days has a kind of boyish energy that is endearing. He is sufficiently wily and exasperating to protect me from sentimentality, but he is so clearly a child of God that I cannot dismiss him. And if I cannot dismiss him, I cannot dismiss his brothers and sisters who live on the street. Anne Frank is my icon for the martyrs of the Holocaust, especially those who never reached full promise. And when I pray for my grandchildren, with their toughness and fragility and their still unblemished perfection, I am using them as icons for *all* children.

It is easy to promise to pray for people, but there is a danger in turning such a pledge into a pious platitude, the equivalent of "Have a nice day." We should be careful to avoid such promises unless we know we will honor them. Besides receiving prayer requests from those close to us, we are often approached by all sorts and conditions of people, some of them highly unlikely, if we are at all recognizable as intercessors. A cross worn round the neck or on a pin may be enough, as is reading a Bible or prayer book in a public place. (Sometimes, on long flights, I am tempted to hide my prayer book in the colorful dust jacket of a bestseller! It's not a generous impulse, and I have not—thus far—succumbed to it.) A clerical collar or a religious habit is a dead giveaway. So I am no longer surprised when strangers, many of them not Christian and possibly not believers at all, ask to be kept in my prayers.

Carmen, the phlebotomist whom I meet regularly at the blood donor center, knows only that I have troublesome small veins and something to do with the church. Despite my explanations she is not ready for female priests, so she calls me "Sister." As she hooks me up to the platelet machine, she asks for my prayers—she is the single mother of an adolescent daughter. Thanks to her, I have learned to turn the "empty" two hours of the donation process into a period of intercession. I close my eyes, start with Carmen, and then move on to the unknown person who will receive my platelets. I have come to look forward to my monthly trips to that impersonal, windowless room as a mini-retreat.

Then there is Rickie, who sits on the retaining wall outside the seminary on sunny days and who proudly introduces me to his best buddy with the words, "He's another wino." Rickie appreciates a sandwich from the deli, but he also asks for my prayers. Maybe he is just trying to make me feel good, somehow as a way of paying for his sandwich, but I take my prayers for him seriously. And there was the ticket salesman in Grand Central Station at rush hour. He looked harassed and impatient, so I was surprised when he shoved my ticket through the little window and said, "Please pray for me." I asked his Christian name and told him that I would pray for him on my journey.

It is important to have a name for the person prayed for. Many street people are nervous of the authorities and anything that smacks of officialdom, so I am careful to assure them that I don't want a surname, "just the name God calls you." One young man, who had obviously once been handsome but was now dirty and wasted, was troubled: "I don't know. I used to have a name, but I think I have lost it." He thought for a moment and added, "But I guess you can call me Richard."

Intercession lends itself to what I call "praying in the cracks." We can pray for others at any time or any place. There is no need for books or special postures or even words. Intercession is a natural kind of prayer for the insomniac or the light sleeper. The closing collect of Compline in the Book of Common Prayer, attributed to Augustine, offers structure:

> Keep watch, dear Lord, with those who work, or watch, or weep this night, and give your angels charge over those who sleep. Tend the sick, Lord Christ; give rest to the weary, bless the dying, soothe the suffering, pity the afflicted, shield the joyous; and all for your love's sake.

This is a prayer to be prayed for taxi drivers, who wonder if their next fare will beat and rob them on the lonely street; for subway crews driving nearly empty trains far underground; for emergency room staffs and rescue squads; for the bakers making tomorrow's bagels and journalists putting together the morning edition. It is a prayer for the grief-stricken widow, for the new parents kept awake by a squalling infant, for the man awaiting surgery in the morning. It is a prayer for the weary derelict sleeping on a sidewalk grating or leaning against a wall in the bus station. It is a prayer for the exhausted woman working a second or third job to make ends meet. We need only let our imaginations and hearts be open, and the empty night hours are no longer empty. Even in solitude we are knit together in community.

Intercessory prayer does not require mobility or even speech. We can pray for others while lying in bed or sitting in a wheelchair. It is a ministry that even the most frail and impaired can exercise. We speak often of ministry *to* the aged and infirm but tend to overlook their gifts and strengths for ministry. In so doing, we are neglecting a potentially powerful group of intercessors. I suspect that many so-called shut-ins feel shut out, even when they appreciate visits and other friendly attention from the parish. I suspect too that the serious pray-ers among them would welcome the opportunity to be put to work, to give as well as to receive.

When I was dividing my time between a nursing home and the hospital just across the street, I sometimes enlisted the help of residents as intercessors. I remember Mrs. Johnson particularly. She was an imposing African-American matriarch, someone whom you would never address informally by her Christian name. Staff and fellow residents were a little afraid of her because her tongue was sharp and her patience short. It was hard to imagine her showing tenderness for anyone. On impulse, I asked her to pray for Towanda, a tiny little girl fighting for life in the neonatal intensive care unit. Mrs. Johnson's face lit up, and she gladly accepted the assignment. Each week when I visited her, her first words would be an inquiry about Towanda—"that precious baby"—followed by the assurance that she was "praying up a storm." Finally, Towanda began to thrive. I do not minimize the skilled care she received in the ICU and her own inborn toughness, but Mrs. Johnson had made a difference. She had held Towanda in her prayers just as tenderly as a grandmother would hold a tiny child in her arms.

Mrs. Johnson unwittingly taught me something about intercession: while she centered her prayer on the frail little girl, she herself was changed. She remained crotchety and demanding to the end—that persona is useful in a nursing home—but it was clear that her imperiousness masked a generous soul. Further, it was clear that despite her failing body she was a woman of great spiritual strength and energy. Although she was surrounded by people, she had been excluded from community, or had perhaps excluded herself. In praying for Towanda, she had brought healing and restoration for herself. The web of connection woven in her prayer anchored both of them. Sometimes I imagined I saw that web, invisible but very strong, stretched across the noisy street separating the hospital and the nursing home.

Some kinds of intercession are difficult. I find it very hard to pray for people whom I have hurt, even when the wounding was inadvertent or unavoidable. Indeed, it is more difficult than praying for those who have hurt me. Part of me wants to deny my responsibility, even to deny that the hurt exists at all. "Okay," says my inner voice, "you've made what amends you could, and it probably wasn't your fault anyway, and you know you couldn't do anything else, so just forget about it." That is a seductive little voice, and as soon as I hear it, I know that it is time for intercession.

Even as we pray for those whom we have hurt, we pray also for those who have hurt us or wish us harm. Jesus' command in the Sermon on the Plain is perfectly clear: "But I say to you that hear, Love your enemies, do good to those who hate you, bless those who curse you, pray for those who abuse you." Here we need to be very cautious. We know the great damage that can be done by premature, coerced "forgiveness." Yet I think everyone, even survivors of physical and sexual abuse, can pray for those who have harmed them. It is enough simply to name the person before God: "Here is X. I have trouble not hating him; in fact, I am pretty sure I *do* hate him. It would be false to say I am praying for him lovingly, because I want to hurt him as much as he has hurt me. I hope that I will heal so that I no longer want to be hurtful. But right now, all I can do is to say his name, to give him over to you."

It is easier to pray for our enemies if they are far away and somewhat faceless; it is harder if they live in our house or share our workplace. As good Christian folk, we can forgive *almost* everyone; the holdouts, interestingly enough, are most often the people closest to us. Surely, we think, God cannot expect us to pray for *them?* Surely I am not expected to pray for the person who is a constant source of irritation or who makes my job ten times harder than it needs to be? Everyone else, of course, but not *them* or *him* or *her.* We all have our holdouts. Most of the time I feel pretty good about my ninety-five percent forgiveness rate and keep the old wounds and hurts and slights alive for the other five percent. It is an interesting exercise to dig into those dark, neglected corners of our souls and identify the holdouts, those people whom we would exclude from our prayers. It is an even more interesting exercise to pray for them!

Deep intercessory prayer has its costs: it opens us to the pain of the world and our own impotence. It is impossible to dismiss callously those for whom we pray. We can no longer allow ourselves the luxury of contempt or vengefulness. Intercession is prayer very much grounded in the here and now: we cannot pray for the world and then turn our backs on the world. We cannot pray for our sisters and brothers and then deny our kinship.

A Ceremony of Kinship

In many congregations the *pedilavium* has become a regular part of the Maundy Thursday liturgy. Even those who don't know the fancy Latin word know the story and the action: after the reading of John's account of Jesus washing Peter's feet is read, the rector or chief pastor kneels down and washes the (usually already washed and clean before leaving home) feet of parishioners. Remember the story: Jesus interrupts the meal to perform a domestic ritual. He gets up from the table, takes off garments that would hamper his movements—the equivalent of taking off a jacket and rolling up one's sleeves—ties a towel around himself like an apron, and starts to wash the feet of his friends. He makes it clear to his disciples that he is giving them an example of servanthood, but there is also something profoundly maternal in his action. I wonder where Jesus learned how to wash those feet. As a guest in many households, he had observed servants doing so, but maybe the memory went deeper. Mothers wash feet and hands and whole bodies. Mothers change diapers. So do grandmothers.

When was the last time you washed someone's feet? Or washed any part of someone? This is an intimate service. Once we are able, we wash ourselves. And we expect others to wash themselves. We prefer it that way. As parents, we wash our babies, then rejoice when those babies get big enough to wash themselves. Now only the truly helpless are washed by others: babies, the sick, the very aged, and the dead. In our culture—except for the babies—this intimate work is deprived of its intimacy, as the care of the sick, the frail aged, and the dead has become an impersonal service to be bought and paid for.

Peter speaks for all of us when he resists. I can almost see him pulling back physically as he says, "You shall never wash my feet." For Jesus' act of hospitality and care calls for humility and submission on both parts. I realized this all too well when as a seminarian I got stuck with the job of recruiting the washees for a Maundy Thursday service. It's much easier to be the one down on the floor with the basin, at least in a tasteful, ceremonial reenactment, than to sit there, wondering where to look (rather like when the violinist comes to your table in a restaurant) and wondering if your feet are really clean and if you might have holes in your socks. Most of us are like Peter: we'd rather do it ourselves. Yet Jesus' action toward his friends is a powerful reminder of the mutual submission and humility inherent in kinship. If we remember his example and incorporate it into ourselves, we'll remember the importance of touch. We'll be willing to touch others and—what is much more difficult—to let ourselves be touched.

I don't wash many feet any more but I did when my work took me among the frail aged who could no longer bend over to care for themselves. Perhaps that is why this story is so vivid for me and why I am impatient with the ritual reenactment on Maundy Thursday. I think of Adelheid, whom I used to visit weekly, a short-tempered old German woman almost immobilized with arthritis. She barely tolerated her caregiver and refused to let the long-suffering woman touch her feet, but as a sign of her trust and affection for me, I was permitted to trim her toenails. I would sit on the floor while her feet soaked in soapy water, then very carefully go to work on her thickened nails. Adelheid would fuss the whole time, warning me not to cut her and complaining about life in general. It took me by surprise one day when I felt her hand gently resting on my shoulder.

The picture of Jesus kneeling before Peter also reminds me of Pauline, who scoured the streets and trash cans for treasure which she stored in her apartment. She had filled the bathtub with old newspapers, to the great neglect of her personal hygiene. I can still see her feet—gnarled, misshapen, with great cracks filled with dirt. When I washed them once, I thought, "I bet even Jesus couldn't get these feet clean! At least not on the first try."

Sometimes we might be called to gird ourselves with a real towel, pour real water into a basin, and kneel before our brother or our sister. But more often we are called to be a serving, humble presence—not to wash real feet, which is in so many ways easier, but to kneel in Christ's place. And sometimes we are called to Peter's place, called to let ourselves be touched and cared for. For the ceremony of footwashing is a kind of circle or dance where we keep changing places; and it is his face we see, whether we are sitting at table or kneeling on the floor. Footwashing is, after all, a family affair.

Love and Kinship

One of my childhood memories is the voice of Franklin Roosevelt in one of his famous Fireside Chats. It was a voice suspiciously eastern and patrician to my family's midwestern, middle-class ears. Even as the country experienced the darkness of economic depression and as the world moved inexorably toward war, he intoned, "We have nothing to fear but fear itself." The Kansas Republicans of my household greeted his words with skepticism; perhaps they would have been more trusting if they recognized the accent of Galilee instead of Groton. But I know now that he was onto something. Letting go of fear might not have revived the stock market or stopped Hitler in his tracks, but it would have freed the nation from the grip of a depression that went far deeper than economic concerns. To be freed from fear is to be restored to vision and mobility. To be freed from fear makes kinship possible.

After so many years, I am still trying to understand the words of John's gospel: "God is love...perfect love casts out fear." The words "God is love" were emblazoned on a banner in my fourth-grade Sunday school room, presented as the answer to everything and a solution to all problems. It is more than a half-century since I sat in that Sunday school room, and sometimes I wish I had never been exposed to that banner. It was like being given the answer before I had articulated or even glimpsed the question, before I had even known that there *was* a question.

I experienced a taste of that love a long time ago, but it has taken me decades to understand it as an icon of the love of God. When I was not quite five, I was dangerously ill. My mother was also ill, so my taciturn Scottish grandfather became my mother. (St. Anne comes in many guises!) He rose before dawn so that he would be sitting at my bedside when I woke. He brought food from home and fed me when I refused hospital fare. When a blood transfusion was ordered, he was the donor. Those were the days of direct transfusion: I have vivid memories of his lying beside me while his blood flowed into my vein. When it was time for the painful changing of dressings, his old hand enveloped mine. I can't recall that he ever said, "Don't be afraid," but he didn't need to. His was a love that cast out fear.

Now that I am a grandparent myself, I have some idea of what those weeks cost him, not only the physical stress of long hours of watching and caring, but the torment of watching my pain and not being able to take it on himself. He was powerless, but in his faithful care of me he became a source of strength.

When we know about this kind of love, we are able to love in a way that, if not perfect, goes a long way toward casting out fear. Spiritually, if not literally, we can love as grandparents. This is a detached love, careless and irresponsible in the best and most literal sense of the word. Parental love is weighted with concerns: Will this child learn the multiplication tables and state capitals? know how to tie his shoes? maybe earn a living some day? By contrast, grandparental love asks for nothing: no conditions are attached. We love because we must. The object of our love is irresistible.

The second half of life brings an awareness of human limitations and a willingness to relinquish control, a letting go of pettiness and fretfulness. Whenever it is achieved, whether remarkably early or just before the end, the loving detachment of the second half of life comes through faithful—and often tedious—living. Eventually, we feel as if we've seen everything. For the spiritually alive, the result is not jaded apathy but a calm detachment.

There were two kindergarten teachers at the little neighborhood school when my children were small. Miss Cameron was young, vivacious, and pretty, while Mrs. Metcalf was not far from retirement. Her clothes could most charitably be described as frumpy, her hair had a wild life of its own, and her glasses usually slipped down to the end of her nose. She always looked a little tired. It was only natural to hope that your child would be assigned to Miss Cameron's room, where youthful liveliness would prevail. Mrs. Metcalf, it was feared by anxious parents, would be rigid and old-fashioned. Instead, the reverse was true. Because she had "seen everything," Mrs. Metcalf was unflappable. At least in the world of five-year-olds, she wasted no energy on faithless fears and worldly anxieties. Rather, she created a secure, coolly loving space in which the children entrusted to her were free to grow.

My friend Sylvia is an even more powerful icon of grandparental love and wisdom. For years she directed a small nursery school. Even when I first knew her, when she must have been in her early fifties, she seemed like an ageless grandmother, Anne embodied. Widely respected and consulted as a professional early childhood educator, she was a true amateur. The love which casts out fear lay at the heart of everything she did. She too, had "seen everything." Nothing seemed to alarm or disgust her. To the best of my knowledge, her school had only two rules: Don't hit people, and don't leave the playground. The asphalt playground and the grassy hill of Sylvia's playground was, in a small way, a re-creation of Anne's enclosed garden of kinship.

When we reach this stage of loving wisdom, not much remains that can disgust or frighten us. We know about frailty, about wounds, and about death. We also know about healing. We are not necessarily fearless, but we have grown immune to those paralyzing "faithless fears and worldly anxieties" that isolate and dehumanize us. We have learned about the possibility, even the joys of openness. To our surprise, we discover that it is all right to let all sorts of people into the garden. Anne's garden is big enough for a large family. Its enclosure suggests shelter, safety, and intimacy. Although it doesn't appear in the Bible, it reminds us of other familiar gardens—Eden before the Fall and the Garden of Paradise promised by Jesus to the penitent thief. It is our home.

Chapter Three

Craft

T hroughout the Middle Ages an astonishing array of men and women looked to St. Anne as patron saint of their craft: sailors, miners, fishermen, and shoemakers. She was patron to all who worked with wood: carpenters, cabinetmakers, and coopers. In parts of France she was known as "the knitting saint," and we are still reminded of her as patron of lacemakers each summer when "her" graceful wildflower blooms along the roadsides and in the fields. Queen Anne's Lace is misnamed: the intricate white blossoms are sacred to God's grandmother, not the queen of England. As the exemplary housewife, St. Anne was also the patron saint of bakers and broommakers, as well as all who worked with thread, yarn, or cloth, not just needleworkers, but also spinners and weavers. And as a good housekeeper, St. Anne was invoked to help find lost objects.

The second half of life is a time of craft and skill, a time when we may reorder and even recreate our lives. It is a crisis, a turning-point, neither good nor bad in itself, a time of cleared vision when we move purposefully off-center and say yes to new ways of being alive. Most of us are far removed from the medieval handiworkers who called upon Anne for help and protection, but we are still artisans bent on crafting our lives, and we find analogies to those occupations under Anne's guardianship.

Spiritually we all work with fibers and fabrics. Spinning and weaving are no longer common household tasks, but they remain powerful metaphors for what we are about. Spinning is humble work, simple and repetitive. In earlier times it was the work of young girls and old women. It can be done mindlessly, with modest equipment. I have a memory, so dim now that I wonder whether it is real or mythic, of Mexican shepherds walking down a dusty road, carrying their spindles and creating yarn as they walked. And it is told of Gandhi that he would spin as a spiritual discipline so that he might remain united with the simple folk who looked to him for leadership.

The product of spinning is a fiber—thread or yarn, the raw material of weaving. If spinning with its circularity suggests a kind of sterile fruitlessness (we speak of spinning our wheels when we are stuck in mud or snow), then weaving is an operation of great complexity. My weaver friend John tells me of the demanding work of setting up the loom, of his careful preparation creating the pattern that will emerge only when the actual weaving has begun. First, he must choose his materials—will he use precious silk or common cotton? He haunts fabric and yarn stores and looks for treasures in suburban yard sales; his greatest satisfaction is transforming something old and discarded into something new and useful. John is particularly fond of old woolen blankets, dyed and torn into strips: "They make great rugs," he tells me. Then there is the intricate work of preparing the loom; this calls for keen eyesight and deft fingers. Finally, when the loom is prepared so that the complex pattern will be revealed, comes the satisfying work of actual weaving. The loom is a large and beautiful instrument, and the weaver must be in harmony with it. John loves his loom and is at home with it, just as a musician must be at home with her instrument.

The technical language of John's craft is filled with strong old Anglo-Saxon words—warp, weft, woof. They are the earthy-sounding words of men and women who work with their hands to create solid, useful objects.

As we craft our lives, there are times of spinning and times of weaving. There are times when we continue to work instinctively, even mechanically, times when our prayer seems circular and mindless. Unlike my remembered shepherd on the dusty road, we cannot see the growing skein of yarn as we continue to walk and spin. There are times too when we are caught up in the tedious yet demanding preparation of the loom, working out a pattern that we cannot see while we strain our eyes and our fingers in the intricate threading of the fibers. This is slow work, infinitely slower than the weaving itself. Finally, there are times of fruition, when the fabric grows before our eyes and the pattern emerges.

I neither spin nor weave, but I find that working with yarn is a satisfying and centering activity. So I crochet—a grandmotherly craft learned in my early childhood from the grandmother who is my namesake. For a long time I forgot about this skill, until I took it up again in my Anne-years. Unlike knitting, which has a certain cachet, crocheting is too old-fashioned even to be quaint. Basically, crochet is the creation of a fabric by the twisting and looping of a single thread by a single needle. Most of the time, it is a "spinning" activity as my fingers move automatically while my mind and eyes are occupied elsewhere. Sometimes it is sensuous: I slow down and savor the color of the yarn, the feel of it in my fingers, the intricacy of the stitch, the contribution of the empty spaces to the emerging pattern. Sometimes it is prayerful; a wise friend has called it my "Protestant rosary," as each stitch becomes a prayer. But in the completed afghan, all the stitches look alike: the prayers and the mindless work of my fingers are identical.

I lack the patience of my weaver friend so I avoid complex patterns, finding variety in color alone. Usually I work with earth tones or grayed hues since the finished products end up as gifts, and my friends are—aesthetically—a conservative lot who choose their accent colors carefully. But from time to time I find myself yearning for vivid colors, for emerald and amethyst, sapphire and ruby. Then I know that it is time for lavishness and abandon. Spiritually, too, there are times for bright colors, times for dancing our prayers instead of murmuring them on our knees. God, I trust, has a greater aesthetic range than we middle-class victims of good taste.

St. Anne can speak to us too as the patron of miners, those who are willing to enter the dark places and look for hidden riches. Mining is traditionally dangerous, unpleasant work. It requires great trust: that the equipment will be reliable, that the air supply will be maintained, and that the mine shaft will not collapse. The miner must descend to the depths and then labor in darkness and cramped spaces. If we are to know ourselves and be truly open to God, we too must be willing to descend to the depths, dig for what is valuable, and then bring it back to the surface. The journey of ever-greater spiritual awareness is not to be undertaken lightly: even as we celebrate being made in God's image, we acknowledge our limitations and our sinfulness. We must be willing to look at ourselves, including and especially those parts which we do not like or which shame us. Like miners working in a dark tunnel, we must be able to recognize rich lodes when we find them, to explore our shadowy depths and then bring the treasure to the surface. We will be enriched, but we will also be changed: that is the risk, not suffocation or being crushed by falling beams.

I sometimes think about the hard work of mining when I meet with people for spiritual direction. In the initial sessions we stay above ground, usually exploring a rather pleasant landscape. But sooner or later, sometimes within a few months and sometimes only after years, it is time for the descent of self-discovery and, ultimately, God-discovery. This is lonely work, for the directee must enter the depths alone. His spiritual companion remains above ground to encourage and support and ultimately to rejoice in the treasure brought to the surface. To be trustworthy, the director must be an experienced miner herself: she must know the underground terrain and have experienced the joys and hardships of laboring there. She must be able to assess the dangers as well: not everyone is ready or strong enough to undertake the descent. Not everyone is called to be a miner.

Finally, we encounter Anne as the exemplary housekeeper who is invoked to find lost objects. She reminds me of the diligent woman in Jesus' parable:

> What woman having ten silver coins, if she loses one of them, does not light a lamp, sweep the house, and search carefully until she finds it? When she has found it, she calls together her friends and neighbors, saying, "Rejoice with me, for I have found the coin that I had lost." (Luke 15:8-9)

What have we lost that needs to be recovered? This loss is not treasure buried deep within, never glimpsed or imagined. The imagery of its discovery is less dramatic: not a descent into the depths of the earth, but rather a vigorous housecleaning. (Is this perhaps another metaphor for at least some aspects of spiritual direction?) Nor is it the inevitable loss that is part of growth: I rejoice that my grandson has learned to read, but I sorely miss the cuddly baby who used to nestle in my lap. Nor is it the voluntary loss, the willing letting-go of whatever impedes and weighs us down: I know that I cannot have a satisfying professional life *and* an immaculate house so—despite the model of Anne as exemplary housekeeper—I have learned to live with dust.

What have we lost that needs to be recovered? In the second half of life, we may have misplaced our spontaneity. We may have forgotten how to play and, given our youth-oriented culture, we may have decided that we are too old and dignified to delight in our bodies.

We may have misplaced our joy in creation. I rejoice in the memory of my father who, when he was close to sixty, would invite me to walk with him barefoot on summer nights so that we could feel the dew on our feet. I must have been about ten. It was a bit of an adventure—people just didn't *do* things like that in the midwest in 1940. But it was also an act of worship, even though no such words were spoken: we were touching God's earth and delighting in God's creation.

Today I came face-to-face with a praying mantis. In my younger days, I didn't like insects and it would never have occurred to me that one might be beautiful. This morning, as the praying mantis let me watch her move slowly up the porch screen, I was struck by the wonder of her. (I knew she was female because her body was heavy with eggs). Her six legs were a marvel of delicate articulation. I watched her for a long time; I wished that I could thank her for her visit and also ask her forgiveness for ever having thought her ugly. This winter I will look for her egg case in the boxwood.

Sometimes it is our very selves that are lost. There is the loss of self from wasted and misdirected energy, from the pursuit of false gods. There is the loss of self in the prison of addiction or after a childhood of injury and abuse. These selves can all be found again. It is no accident that the story of the woman searching for the lost coin in Luke follows the parable of the lost sheep, and immediately precedes the story of the prodigal son. What we have lost and what we ultimately find—as we descend to the depths like miners and scour the house like good housekeepers—is ourselves. Like the prodigal son, we "come to ourselves."

Crafting Our Lives

One definition of spirituality might well be "crafting our lives." To live as fully human and as children of God requires the same kind of care that the master craftsman brings to his work. It is slow work with lots of time spent learning simple things. We forget how hard we worked as young children to deal with the intricacies of sphincter muscles! We learn to walk upright, to use language, eventually to tie our shoes. We become at home with a rich variety of materials and learn to use many tools. If we are true artisans rather than day laborers, we bring real love and commitment to the work at hand. We care about what we are doing because we know that it matters.

Tom has taught me a great deal about the thoughtful crafting of the second half of life. Young enough to be my son, he had been my colleague briefly and then we lost touch. I remembered him as energetic and handsome, with a wicked sense of humor. Not long ago we met and talked, probably the first real conversation despite our months of working together. Tom is thin now; he moves and looks like an old man. The AIDS virus has taken its toll. He talked about the gifts of time and energy, how precious they had become to him. "I want beautiful things near me now," he said. "I've always loved beautiful things, but never had time to pay attention, or maybe I didn't want to spend the money. But now somehow it matters. I have to laugh at myself—I polish my grandmother's tea service and rub lemon oil into her cherrywood desk. It makes me feel connected, like I have a home even though I've had to move to a small apartment—I couldn't afford my old place, and I couldn't keep it up anyway. This one is tiny, but I've cared about every inch of it. I want things around me that matter. And I'm learning not to waste my strength. If I rest every afternoon, I can enjoy the remainder of the day." I sensed that he chose the word "enjoy" with great care and understood its depth.

In his wise book *Care of the Soul*, Thomas Moore observes that

> Plato used the expression *techne tou biou,* which means "the craft of life." When *techne* is defined with sufficient depth, it refers not just to mechanical skills and instruments but to all kinds of artful managing and careful shaping. For now, we can say that care of the soul requires a special crafting of life itself, with an artist's sensitivity to the way things are done.[1]

Unfortunately, for many of us the root *techne* has lost its richness and mystery. Most of the English words derived from it have an aura of dry remoteness: technology, technocrat, technique, technicolor are all impersonal words, untouched by human hands.

"Craft," on the other hand, is a strong and vital word, retaining the earthiness of the Anglo-Saxon. It can also have negative connotations: craftiness can suggest deviousness and conniving. But the word also has connotations of canniness, of grasping the situation clearly, knowing how things are done, and then quietly getting on with it. This craftiness can be an Anne-quality, reflecting the practical wisdom of old age.

Agatha Christie has given us an engaging exemplar of craft in her Miss Marple, a canny old woman who uses her harmless appearance to great advantage. People see her as a pleasant grandmotherly presence, always knitting fluffy indeterminate garments for babies. Her shrewd tenaciousness makes officialdom nervous; then, when she has yet again solved the mystery for them, they grudgingly acknowledge her gifts. Miss Marple relies on her long life experience to make connections; her denouements typically begin with the statement that the situation, however gory and entangled, reminds her of something that happened in her quiet village of

---

1   Thomas Moore, *Care of the Soul* (New York: HarperCollins, 1992), p. xvii.

St. Mary Mead. The connection may not be clear to anyone else, but to her it is obvious. A grandmother without ever being a mother, she has a special affinity for the young, who trust her and take her seriously when those in authority minimize her. While she is presented as an aged virgin who has led a blameless and not very interesting life, she has an uncanny sensitivity to evil. She is fearless, perhaps because she knows that she is going to die soon, whether she guards her life jealously or chooses to risk boldly. Miss Marple is not above dissembling, encouraging people to minimize and misunderstand her. She is deceptively gentle so that people tell her their secrets and let her see their true selves. She has no need to flaunt her wisdom, for she is not interested in celebrity. Miss Marple would make a fine spiritual director if she were not so busy solving crimes; in her way, she is a consummate craftswoman.

While it can suggest cunning or strength (the German word is *Kraft*), most commonly "craft" suggests a useful skill acquired through experience. The word has a pleasantly archaic sound, and whenever I hear it, I think of my German grandfather. One of the treasured implements in my kitchen is a wooden potato masher, carved from hickory (or is it chestnut?) by him over one hundred years ago. I never knew Georg Beltz—he died long before I was born. I have one picture of him, uncomfortable in an unaccustomed "good" suit, his beard long and white, as he faced the camera in the once-in-a-lifetime ordeal of being photographed. My grandfather was a farmer who came to Missouri as a young man to avoid conscription by Bismarck's army. He never had much money, and he was used to making what he needed with his hands.

The potato masher is a simple thing, a shaftlike handle with a substantial knob at the end. The hard wood is worn to a satiny smoothness. The little implement is balanced; it feels good to hold. It is—in the truest sense of the word—handy. I rarely mash potatoes any more, but we are fond of Middle

Eastern food, and my grandfather's rural "craft" is just right for turning chick peas into hummus. On a particularly busy day one of my children asked why I didn't use the electric food processor for this work, and without thinking I replied, "I'm in a hurry, and that gadget is just too much trouble." That was true, but when I reflected on the incident, I knew that I also loved the deep satisfaction of the carved wood in my hand and the sense of connection with the kind-looking old man who had made it for his overworked wife.

True craft is slow work, requiring patience. You need to know the material: is it right for the intended purpose? Will it hold up to hard use? Beauty almost always accompanies true craft, whether the material is wood, cloth, yarn, or pottery, but I doubt that my grandfather was thinking about beauty as he transformed a sturdy little piece of wood into a useful object.

Craft is often the work of leisure. I am sure that my grandfather carved the potato masher after a long day of work in the fields and the barns, just as my grandmother made quilts and rag rugs after her "real" work was done. It must have been the most pleasurable time of the day for them, just to sit and rest their tired bodies while their hands created objects of usefulness and beauty.

The Practice of Craft

While she may produce works of great beauty, the craftswoman is only incidentally an artist, for her skill is not dependent on special gifts or artistic ability in the commonly accepted sense. Mastery of a craft is possible for all, not just a specially gifted few; it is the fruit of patience and steady, often tedious practice. I learned this again recently when I acquired a NordicTrack and tried to imitate what looked so easy on the video. It took time and great concentration to make my arms and legs move in unaccustomed patterns, to say nothing of staying upright on my fake skis. There was—and is—nothing exhilarating about the dogged effort required. I know too that

that dogged effort will bear fruit if I can just hang in and endure the dullness of repeated movement that seems to go nowhere.

Children are expected to endure the tedium of practice, whether it be learning the multiplication tables or rules of grammar and spelling. Music lessons, too, are commonly the province of children. I remember myself as a conscientious child, playing endless scales the requisite number of times and hating every note. I wanted to make music, spectacular music, with eyes shut and fingers flying over the keys; instead, I struggled with fingering and remembering my sharps and flats. My piano playing never approached art, but when I returned to it in middle age, it took on qualities of a well-loved craft. Maybe because I now understood something of the fruits of faithfulness and practice, I did not tire of playing same Bach fugue over and over—trying to get it right, trying to make my fingers do what they were supposed to, trying to dig into the mystery of the little round black marks on the page.

As adults, we don't "have time" for such commitment to repetitive work that leads nowhere quickly. We like quick fixes—cassettes that promise to teach us a new language painlessly in just a few hours are an amusing symbol of our attraction to speeded-up approaches. Anyone who has mastered a second language knows the long work of painstaking trial and error, the discovery of nuance, and finally the entry into new patterns of thought.

I am delighted that I do not have to carve my kitchen implements out of hard blocks of wood. I have happily forgotten the intricate steps of ironing starched cotton shirts, a part of every young woman's education when I was growing up. I rejoice that my husband does not expect me to knit his socks. The wonderful variety of New York bakeries and my own busy schedule relieve me of breadmaking, a craft I enjoyed when my children were small. But at the same time I regret the loss of patience and dedication that made me, in a small way, a craftswoman.

To be a craftsman is to live in the everyday world and to be devoted to the ordinary. Craft is always purposeful; its aim is always the creation of something *useful*. My maternal grandmother was an expert quiltmaker; she turned scraps of cloth into exquisite works of art. She had, perhaps, an artist's eye but the busy fingers of a craftswoman. It was she who taught me to sew with tiny, regular stitches. She was unimpressed by the surface appearance, but always turned the work over to inspect the hidden side: anybody, she maintained, could turn out something that merely looked good. She intended her quilts to be used, to be placed on beds to keep people warm. Her great-grandchildren own them now and treat them as sacred objects, art to be cherished and hung on the wall, and I'm not sure whether my grandmother would be pleased or irritated!

Beauty in craft lends delight and grace, but it is always secondary to the true aim of craft: to create something useful and usable. The intention is always humble: to do the work well. This means honoring and knowing the raw materials; there is no place for plastic and Velcro in the craftswoman's workshop. Similarly she knows and honors the instruments of her craft. St. Benedict's Rule talks about the stewardship of tools, however common and simple they may be: they are to be treated with the same reverence as the sacred vessels of the altar.

Asceticism

We live in a culture that is uneasy with asceticism. If we mention it at all, the very word smacks of unwholesome medieval practices of self-denial and self-inflicted pain. Yet this is ironic, for we are a people preoccupied with ascetical practices, not all of them good for us. I think of this when I pass runners in the park, their faces distorted and strained to the point of exhaustion. If I merely saw their pictures, I would assume that they were torture victims! And I think of this when I spend time with friends who have dedicated their lives to climbing the corporate ladder: they have given up close personal relationships, even modest leisure, and spontaneity as they devote themselves single-mindedly to their work. Theirs is an asceticism almost as harsh and depriving as that of the abbas of the fourth-century Egyptian desert, but they don't know it.

From time to time people wince when I tell them that I am a professor of ascetical theology. They wonder whether I teach seminarians and directees how to sleep on beds of nails. Hair shirts are out-of-fashion, but certainly anything to do with asceticism must be disagreeable and uncomfortable. Surely, they think, I am not gaunt enough or wretched enough to do my job well!

Ascetical theology is practical and down-to-earth; it is about living in the here and now, most particularly about living in relationship to God. It is concerned with how we live out our professed beliefs, how we sanctify the ordinary, how we cultivate awareness of God in the small and everyday. As the root of the word suggests, *ascesis*—training—is what it is all about. Lurid stories of harsh and excessive disciplines practiced by our medieval forebears make entertaining reading, but they miss the point. It is time to reclaim asceticism as something healthy, desirable, and God-oriented.

In his first letter to the Corinthians, Paul offers the foundational text for all ascetical practice:

> Do you not know that in a race the runners all compete, but only one receives the prize? Run in such a way that you may win it. Athletes exercise self-control in all things; they do it to receive a perishable wreath, but we an imperishable one. So I do not run aimlessly, nor do I box as though beating the air; but I punish my body and enslave it, so that after proclaiming to others I myself should not be disqualified. (1 Corinthians 9:24-27)

Paul's words make it clear that the intent of asceticism is neither masochistic nor punitive. As the athletic imagery indicates, it is a matter of being in optimum condition for running the race. Implicit in this is the idea of self-control: whatever training regimen we might undertake is freely chosen, not as a gratuitous hardship but as the best means of getting and staying in shape for the marathon. In other words, we exercise self-control as a matter of stewardship of resources and determining priorities.

As I search for models in the tradition, I am attracted to the asceticism implicit in the Benedictine Rule. Even though it was designed for monks more than a millennium ago, the Rule speaks in practical terms to those of us who seek guidance in crafting the second half of our lives. Writing about the everyday conduct of life in community, Benedict repeatedly reminds us that God is to be encountered in the small and the ordinary, in the workplace as well as at the altar. That does not mean that Benedict ignores the importance of our intellects, for a second feature of his Rule is the attention he pays to learning. Just as we may relegate the tedium of repetitive practice to children (good for them, we think, but unnecessary and diminishing for us), so too we commonly see study as the task of youth. And we want to be able to measure progress by grades passed, marks given, and degrees received. But the Rule sees ongoing study—serious study, not merely reading bestsellers—as part of life's work.

For us, even to keep abreast of current events seems an impossible task, so we fall back on television news or news magazines such as *Time* and *Newsweek*. There is so much to know, so much to study that our brains are either reeling or totally shut down. Yet it is especially important that we be attentive to the kind of study Benedict had in mind, namely, to apply our minds—as well as our emotions—to our relationship with God. A healthy asceticism calls us to intellectual engagement: narrowly, with matters of our faith and, more generally, with the world we inhabit. It is an impossible task, at least one that is never finished; but that should not deter our beginning. Study is a craft that merits our devotion.

Finally, I am struck by Benedict's emphasis on work. As a people, we are often so identified with our jobs that we forget what a relatively recent phenomenon this is. Indeed, one of Benedict's claims to distinction is his elevation of work, menial work, to a high place in the human value system. His inclusion of manual labor as part of the Rule was a way of sanctifying the ordinary, of reminding us of the (at least potential) holiness of the material. In our own century, Gandhi was very "Benedictine" when he said:

> Whether you wet your hands in the water basin, fan the fire with the bamboo bellows, set down endless columns of figures at a desk, labor in the rice fields with your head in the burning sun and your feet in the mud, or stand at work before the smelting furnace, so long as you do not do all this with just the same religiousness as if you were monks praying in a monastery, the world will never be saved.

In Benedict's day, this new emphasis on work was important in the achievement of balance: the tasks of everyday living were no longer something to be avoided by those able to relegate them to others. Rather, Benedict regarded work as an integral part of life for all. But we are a people whose lives are out of balance in a different way. We define ourselves by our jobs, and we name ourselves by our occupations. And, as I have already noted, we bring an ascetic intensity to the corporate climb that rivals the austere practices of medieval monastics!

The qualities of true craft—unhurriedness, patience, joy in creating objects of usefulness and quality, freedom to focus on one thing at a time—seem alien to me most mornings when I attack my cluttered desk. Conversations with my colleagues sometimes threaten to turn into a competition to see which of us is the busiest. That is why it took me by surprise when a wise friend once pointed out that mindless activity for its own sake, filling up our time so that God is crowded out, is none other than the sin of sloth. "Sloth" has such a lazy, inert sound to it. I can recognize and acknowledge my slothfulness if I spend hot summer afternoons in the hammock, reading and dozing over forgettable novels. It is more uncomfortable to realize that the sin of sloth, the *acedia* so dreaded by the desert abbas and ammas, has slithered into my life when I find myself too busy to pray, to hold still even for a moment, too busy to listen to the silence. Not only have I crowded God out of my little life; in my self-importance I have tried to become God.

Crafting a Rule of Life

Not long ago my seven-year-old grandson asked if he might play my piano. I gave the usual cautions about having clean hands and a gentle touch, then—remembering my own early days—asked if he wanted me to show him how to make a tune. He declined indignantly and assured me that he knew how to play. He is a bright child, but no infant Mozart, so the result of his intensely concentrated effort remained cacophony. He was frustrated that no song emerged, but he couldn't believe that music had *rules*.

His considerably older grandfather exhibits a similar reluctance to submit to the discipline of a rule in the kitchen. He wants to cook and insists that *everybody* can cook—there's nothing to it. The teacher in me wants to give demonstrations and suggest books; the craftswoman in me is indignant. There *are* rules and they should be followed. At the very least, they must be known before they can be disregarded. Julia Child, a great icon of the second half of life, was always endearingly easygoing in her televised kitchen, but her followers knew that her seemingly casual approach to her craft was the fruit of a lifetime's acceptance of its rules. A rule provides a basis, a continuity for craft—whether we are talking about chopping vegetables or crafting a life. Craft requires discipline, and craft requires the almost daily exercise of staying in practice. Craftsmen are set free to do their best work by submitting to rules.

When people come to me for spiritual direction, I always assume that, at some level, they are concerned with formulating a rule of life. They may not use these words, since the term is traditionally associated with religious or monastic spirituality and has a medieval aura about it. But they are concerned with the stewardship of their time and energy (as well as their substance) and are looking for help in shaping their days. Most commonly, our discussion begins with the question of time: how can they find time for prayer and contemplation in a crowded schedule?

While most people go through life without thinking of it, we all have a rule of life, a pattern for our days reflecting our deepest beliefs. For fifteen years I lived next door to Wilbur, who was not religiously observant and who had probably never heard of a rule of life. Yet there was something almost monastic about his faithfulness to his unwritten rule: he rose every morning at 6:30, left his house at 7:00, and returned home from work by 3:30. In the summer he then sat on his porch; in the winter he sat in the living room. He drank beer until he was almost unconscious and then somehow put himself to bed. He had held the same job for years and never missed going to work. He was a quiet, affable neighbor; his yard was always neatly kept. Even if he never articulated it to himself, Wilbur had an austere and workable rule of life. Unfortunately, his god lived in a bottle and eventually killed him.

It is not enough to live by an unconscious rule. For Christians, there are predictable components related to prayer and worship. A typical "bare bones" rule of life would deal with such questions as, how and when do I pray? What are my rhythms of corporate and solitary prayer? What is the place of the sacraments in my life? How often do I join in the celebration of the eucharist? If it is part of my tradition, how often do I avail myself of the sacrament of reconciliation?

I think a good rule would go beyond and build upon these bare essentials, for they *are* essentials. It would include a commitment to the guidance and companionship of spiritual direction or spiritual friendship. Given the complexity and overstimulation of life in the industrialized West, it would encourage the cultivation of simplicity. This is by no means the same as harsh self-denial, but rather an attempt to reduce the spiritual and material clutter that choke off our growth.

Further, a good rule would be committed to generosity; this would go beyond the simple allocation of money for charitable giving to include gifts of self and service. Baron von Hügel instructed Evelyn Underhill to work in a soup kitchen as a way of grounding her spirituality; we too need our "soup kitchens"—whatever form they may take—to keep us honest and embodied. I am always uneasy with directees who have cut themselves off from the pain and grittiness of the world around them and who seem to have no impulse even to *see* the needs of others. For those living in urban centers, the opportunities for service are myriad. For those in gentler places, where need can be masked or denied, the opportunities are still present. Miss Marple would be able to point them out in a flash, even in St. Mary Mead.

A good rule also includes provision for self-care. Again and again, I talk with people who are very specific about patterns and disciplines for their devotional lives but neglectful of their physical and emotional selves. This part of the rule is concerned with re-creation, and each individual knows best how he or she can be re-created. Does time need to be built in for study? music? solitude? manual labor? fasting? (In her book *Fullness of Life,* Margaret Miles offers the provocative suggestion of fasting from the media.) The sedentary need to include regular exercise as a holy obligation, and the variously addicted need to look hard at the idols that have crept into their lives. Workaholics must build a sabbath into their rule, and clergy should remember that the sabbath can be observed on any day of the week.

The purpose of the rule is to keep us clear and attentive, to enable us to live contemplatively in the midst of activity. The temptation, of course, is to be overambitious and to set ourselves impossible goals—and then to fail. There is also the danger that the structure will become an end in itself, so that our spirituality becomes joyless, life-denying, and self-centered. Particularly in regard to "spiritual disciplines," less is frequently more. A good rule can set us free to be our true and best selves. It is a working document, a kind of spiritual budget, not carved in stone but subject to regular review and revision. It should support us, but never constrict us.

I usually suggest that a comprehensive rule of life be structured according to a four-fold pattern of relationships: first and most obvious is our relationship to God, then to others, to the whole of creation, and to our own deepest selves. Whatever shape our rule may assume, our relationship with God lies at its heart. In the name of faithfulness and piety, we are often in danger of getting stuck in outworn patterns and resisting the surprises and challenges of growth.

Yet this relationship is not static, mechanical, or reducible to a formula. Nor is it always a comfortable relationship, and certainly not one to be taken casually. As we are reminded in the letter to the Hebrews:

> The word of God is living and active, sharper than any two-edged sword, piercing until it divides soul from spirit, joints from marrow; it is able to judge the thoughts and intentions of the heart. And before him no creature is hidden, but all are naked and laid bare to the eyes of the one to whom we must render an account. (Hebrews 4:12-13)

This is a God who makes demands, a God to whom all hearts are open, all desires known, from whom no secrets are hid. If we let ourselves become ossified in our rule—I *must* read the morning office because I have always done so, even though something deep within tells me to sit in contemplative silence for half an hour—we risk using it as a defense against growth and turning our rule into an idol.

Then we need to consider the people in our lives. As a parent, what does my rule say about my relationship with my children? Do I listen to my child? Do I accord him the dignity I accord all other human beings? Do I leave her space to develop into her own person? Parents always walk a narrow line: too much attention and involvement is smothering, too little is neglect. Here, as elsewhere in the rule, it is important to be aware of areas of potential disproportion. And as a husband or wife, how can I shape my rule to honor my marriage vows? Has my work become a jealous mistress or lover? Where do aging parents, young grandchildren, and other relatives fit into my rule? It may seem trivial to include a weekly phone call or visit, but such a commitment is far from inconsequential. The rule also should take into account those others with whom we are in daily contact—our colleagues in the workplace, our neighbors, even those who seem to have been put on this earth just to give us trouble.

Looking at our relationship to all of creation can be a daunting undertaking. This part of the rule forces us to think about politics, economics, and the environment, huge areas that seem beyond our control. One of the most difficult parts for me is my commitment to be responsibly informed about situations far from home: there is so much to know, and I find it easier simply to give up than to persevere. How can I craft my life to assure a Christ-centered response to famine in sub-Saharan Africa or the denuding of the Amazon rain forest? And while I am convinced the membership in Amnesty International is a step in the right direction, where are my areas of deep unconsciousness regarding torture and oppression? Matters are much simpler when they can be dealt with locally. So according to my rule, at the corner market I risk the disapproval of the checkout lady and virtuously refuse paper or plastic, packing my groceries into a net bag.

Finally, the rule relates to our deepest selves. It is a truism, articulated in various times and in various ways by the mystics, that we cannot know and love God until we know and love our own selves. Unless we are committed to self-knowledge and the self-care already discussed, we are enmeshed in self-deception. In *The Screwtape Letters,* C. S. Lewis gives a delightful picture of such a deluded seeker, in a passage where the devil Screwtape gives advice to his devil-in-training nephew Wormwood:

> Keep his mind off the most elementary duties by directing it to the most advanced and spiritual ones. Aggravate that most useful human characteristic, the horror and neglect of the obvious. You must bring him to a condition in which he can practise self-examination for an hour without discovering any of those facts about himself which are perfectly clear to anyone who has ever lived in the same house with him or worked in the same office.[2]

"The horror and neglect of the obvious" is not commonly listed among the cardinal sins, but it can turn an otherwise balanced rule of life into an absurd and deceitful document.

To formulate the rule of life that I have proposed calls for a careful review of all facets and corners of one's life. It is a two-leveled work, for it is simultaneously general and specific. Obviously, the resulting document would be very detailed and much too long to have at one's fingertips. Nevertheless, it is a useful exercise to survey one's life from time to time and then work out such a rule, concentrating in turn on each of the four areas and noting areas of disproportion and potential sinfulness. Writing it all down is important, since

---

2   C. S. Lewis, *The Screwtape Letters* (New York: Macmillan, 1962), p. 16.

writing sharpens the focus and forces us to say what we mean. Then we sit lightly with it. It is absurd to picture ourselves consulting a bulky, multi-paged text with paragraphs and subparagraphs. The essentials will be firmly implanted within us.

A Rule of Play

In the Blue Ridge I love to watch the young calves in a nearby mountain pasture: they run with abandon and without apparent purpose, wheel about in sharp turns, are joined by their fellows in a glorious romp, and then stop as suddenly as they started. Then I look at their mothers—great, stolid beasts—and wonder what has happened. When did the gracefulness and grace-filledness disappear? When did the joy of cool air and soft turf and blue sky cease to exhilarate? When did it stop being fun to run as fast as they could, just for the fun of it? But surely, I think, as the cows and I ruminate together, this has nothing to do with me. Unlike the immobile bovine matrons on the other side of the fence, surely *I* haven't forgotten how to play.

Our need for true play is often neglected in a rule of life. By the time we reach the second half of life the re-creative art of play can be crowded out and forgotten, but I am convinced that play has an important place in our ascetical practices. If we intend to maintain ourselves in good condition—physically and emotionally, to say nothing of spiritually—we dare not let our inborn gift for play atrophy and wither away from lack of exercise. We dare not let ourselves become ponderous, too heavy to move. Play exists for its own sake. Play is for the moment; it is not hurried, even when the pace is fast and timing *seems* important. When we play, we also celebrate holy uselessness. Like the calf frolicking in the meadow, we need no pretense or excuses. Work is productive; play, in its disinterestedness and self-forgetting, can be fruitful.

A four-year-old friend recently reminded me of the sheer abundance of play. We had just finished our very wholesome meal with a wholesome dessert of fresh fruit. He then offered to serve a second dessert and fetched his toy dishes. "Have some chocolate pudding," he said. "It has chocolate chips in it, too." "Could I have a little whipped cream on top?" I asked. "Sure, all you want." We enjoyed our pretend desserts, and then I asked for seconds. "Sure," he said, "we've got enough for seconds. Or thirds. Or fourths." There is indeed a prodigality in play, a kind of breathtaking limitlessness. (God set us a good example by creating over 900,000 species of insects, including a few I could do without and some we haven't yet identified.)

For all its lightness, play is intensely serious business; just watch the concentration children bring to it. Art is a kind of play, and so is liturgy. Play—holy play—is what keeps us humble and keeps us human. Without it, we tend to become ponderous, convinced that God can't run the operation unless we are there to cover for him. When I find myself acting like God's capable but officious administrative assistant, correcting his mistakes and explaining what he really means, I know that I have lost my sense of holy play.

Decades ago I taught English to a room full of dignified Japanese gentlemen. Despite all my efforts and their own hard work, some of them never managed to distinguish the sounds of "l" and "r." For them, it was simply not a meaningful distinction. I remember Mr. Matsuzawa and Mr. Nishimura and all the others when I reflect on the holiness of "playing." For them, it would sound just like "praying."

Stripping Down

As I write, it is early October, and the Christmas catalogues have begun to flood my mailbox. I wonder what an extraterrestrial would think of the variety and number of *things*—beautiful, bizarre, useful, useless—that I am invited to

buy or give to others. Most of us enjoy more than a Benedictine sufficiency; we are glutted with things. Even the North
American poor are "rich" in things, if only empty aluminum
cans and styrofoam cups.

We like to talk about simplicity. Last year as I prepared to
spend a sabbatical term in my Blue Ridge hollow, I went on at
length to a colleague about the joys of "a radically simplified
environment." No television, no car, the nearest fax machine
in the county seat twelve miles away, wood stoves, my desk
made of an old door on two sawhorses, a dress code of ancient jeans and sweatshirts—I painted a picture of unadorned
living right out of the nineteenth century. "But of course," I
went on, "I'll need to take a few things with me, just my lap-
top computer, an external disk drive for backups, a mini-
printer, plenty of books, also plenty of tapes for my
Walkman—and my Visa card." My friend merely raised his
eyebrows, and I had the grace to blush.

Our way of life is in stark contrast to the gospel instruction
to travel light:

> Go on your way. See, I am sending you out like lambs into
> the midst of wolves. Carry no purse, no bag, no sandals.
> (Luke 10:3-4)

There is inescapable irony in this gospel when it is read in an
average congregation on an average Sunday morning. In a
way, we are not so different from the people whom I see on
the streets of New York wearing layers of ragged and ill-
matched clothes, even in the hottest weather, pushing their
possessions before them in metal shopping carts "liberated"
from some grocery store—old styrofoam cups, more clothes,
small electrical appliances that no longer work even if the
present owner had an outlet to plug it in, broken umbrellas,
every imaginable sample of the detritus of the city streets.
Their whole identity is in that shopping cart stuffed with plas-

tic bags of trash, and their whole protection is layer upon layer of castoff, filthy clothing.

One of the friends whom I hope to meet in heaven is Pauline, an affluent bag lady. She had some income and a potentially pleasant apartment in a large, almost elegant building. But she was driven to accumulate, to surround herself with everything she could glean from the trash containers in her neighborhood. When I first met her, I assumed that she was impoverished and lived on the street; she was layered in unwashed clothes and dragging several bulging shopping bags. As I got to know her better, I realized that she was a prisoner of her accumulated trash; she needed it to feel safe, but there was never enough, so she had to keep gathering more.

The situation became critical when the management of her building sought to evict her as a fire hazard. Another friend and I begged her to let us throw away just the old newspapers and used styrofoam cups. We promised to be careful and to discard nothing of value. Pauline agreed, but she wept as she watched us make trip after trip to the incinerator. When we had finally completed our hard work, her apartment was spacious and numerous treasures had come to light—pretty dishes, family photographs, and forgotten books. We had saved her from eviction, but both of us knew that she would be back on the sidewalk, combing through the trash, by the next morning.

My genuine fondness for Pauline was mingled with impatience that she—a bright and advantaged woman—couldn't get her act together. But in my heart I knew that she was who she was and also that my discomfort came largely from seeing myself mirrored in her. For we can and do so layer ourselves. We may do it more subtly, without neglecting grooming or hygiene, but spiritually we all have our defensive accumulations of precious trash.

Just a quick look at history (or the daily paper) can remind us how fragile our carefully constructed shelters and defenses can be. The rich nineteenth-century culture of the German and Austrian Jewish communities was swept away almost overnight when Hitler came to power. The survivors were scattered to alien places, forced to build new lives and new identities from nothing. The less fortunate faced degradation, unspeakable suffering, and death. Before the Holocaust they must have felt, like most of us, that their lives were stable and their future assured. Like us, they had houses, work, bank accounts, families, and friends. Anne Frank and I were born in the same year, both with fathers named Otto, into families that had much in common. As bright and competitive little girls, I am sure that we would have been arch-rivals in school and probably would not have liked each other very much. Why did the security of my early childhood continue, while hers was destroyed?

It is no accident that the Bible is full of departures, that the journey motif has become a cliché. We cannot expect permanence: our lives are made up of arrivals and departures, departures and arrivals. Even if we live in the same dwelling all our lives, we must keep repeating the drama of the Exodus. We may share the homesickness of the Israelites, who found that even slavery began to look good:

> And the Israelites also wept again, and said, "If only we had meat to eat! We remember the fish we used to eat in Egypt for nothing, the cucumbers, the melons, the leeks, the onions, and the garlic; but now our strength is dried up, and there is nothing at all but this manna to look at." (Numbers 11:4b-6)

Departure and arrival, packing and unpacking are a powerful spiritual discipline. Preparation for even a short trip can be an exercise in asceticism, and moving to a new house is spiritually as well as physically a major undertaking. To face newness, growth, and change, we are forced to take stock of ourselves and our lives, to order our priorities and our loves.

Some years ago, when I left the neighborhood where I had lived for twenty years, I was forced to decide: what was valuable, and what was trash? What should be carried with me, and what should be discarded? Unlike the people of Israel, I had time for a yard sale.

Etty Hillesum, the remarkable Dutch Jew who became known to us a few years ago when fragments of her journals were published as *An Interrupted Life*, knew that she was about to be sent to a concentration camp. And she knew that she could take with her one small rucksack, perhaps about one cubic foot of possessions to sustain her as she entered hell. In her mind, she planned and pondered, mentally packed and unpacked that small bag, finally deciding on a Bible, a volume of her favorite poems by Rilke, a bottle of aspirin, an extra sweater, and a chocolate bar. Modest equipment for such a journey, but perhaps as good as anything else.

Whether death is approaching us or we are approaching death, the end of life demands its own *ascesis*. Etty knew this instinctively, as she struggled to define what was valuable to her and what sustained her, symbolized in the meager contents of her knapsack. A stripping-down, a letting-go was inevitable as even small freedoms were curtailed and transport to the death camp came inexorably closer.

Most of us resist even the thought of embracing powerlessness; we prefer action. Ultimately, however, the asceticism for the second half of life—the training program to get in shape, if you will—is linked to powerlessness, even to passivity. The English Franciscan W. H. Vanstone has written compellingly of this holy passivity in a deceptively simple little book called *The Stature of Waiting*. Drawing chiefly on the gospels of John and Mark, he points out the dramatic division of Jesus' ministry into two distinct parts. The Jesus whom most of us prefer to emulate, certainly the Jesus to whom we are drawn, is active: he preaches, teaches, argues, travels, heals, prays, and feasts. Grammatically, he is the subject, not the object, of most sentences. But when he is arrested—given over, handed up—he becomes passive. After that, he speaks very little and is *done unto*. As Vanstone puts it:

> When we speak of the passion of Jesus we should be re-
> ferring not to His suffering, not to the pains which He en-
> dured or the cruel manner in which he was treated by the
> hands of men, but simply to the fact that He was exposed
> to those hands, affected by whatever those hands might
> do. With this understanding of the word "passion," we may
> say that the moment when Jesus was refreshed by a moist
> sponge was as truly a part of His passion as the moment
> when He was scourged or the moment when his hands
> were nailed to the cross.[3]

It is this being "done unto" that goes against our grain, even when it is benevolent. We resist it, perhaps rightly, as long as we can, and ultimately see it as defeat. Yet if Christ's life is a model and a pattern, we are impelled to see the certainty, indeed the ultimate rightness of this stage of life.

Of course, we can move from action to passivity in the twinkling of an eye; an automobile accident, a fall, an act of violence can deliver us up to the hands of others. Minor, even trivial illnesses provide a foretaste: the incapacitating viruses that lay us low and deprive us of our dignity, if only for twenty-four hours. I don't mind wearing glasses for reading, but it hurts my vanity to admit that I don't hear quite so well as I used to, or that my right knee objects when I kneel. When I move beyond my vanity, I know that there is nothing that I can do about it as I move steadily toward that part of the *Imitatio Christi* that I would most like to avoid.

What can those in the second half of life, indeed those in the second half of the second half, build into their rule to em-

---

3   W. H. Vanstone, *The Stature of Waiting* (New York: Seabury, 1983), pp. 30-31.

brace what will come? How can we practice? What spiritual muscles must we stretch and strengthen?

As we prepare for our departures, both literal and spiritual, we take hold of each possession and ask: Will I be sustained or pulled under by this attachment? It is a time to take everything out and examine it. This may not be comfortable—it can be profoundly unsettling—but as Christians we live, or should live, much of our life at the edge. It is the time to sort ourselves out, not merely our old socks and sweaters and everything else we drag through life. It is a time to sort things out and then, like Etty, to pack our bag.

Chapter Four

Healing, Wholeness, and Harvest

B y the late Middle Ages, Anne was a beloved and much invoked saint: besides being patron to a variety of workers of craft, she was called upon for maternal, indeed grandmotherly support by those yearning for healing and wholeness. St. Anne was protector of the poorest of the poor as well as of the sick: shelters and hospitals commonly bore her name. Her help was invoked against the plague. Because the legends told of her long childlessness before the miraculous birth of Mary, she was also the patron saint of the barren: unmarried girls prayed for her help in finding husbands and infertile women turned to her for aid in becoming pregnant. At the same time, she was patron of the fruitful—of pregnant women, women in childbirth, and the harvest. In a patriarchal church she was revered as a tasteful and orthodox earth mother, promising fertility and abundance.

A rich constellation of words and themes cluster around this aspect of Anne, one that has special significance for the second half of life. The relationship between "heal" and "whole" is obvious, although we may overlook their intimate connection and forget that the purpose of healing is not a *cure* but rather the restoration of wholeness. Also related is "hale," which has a pleasantly archaic ring. "Hale" is usually found in company with "hearty." (These are definitely words for the second half of life: I can't recall hearing a winsome infant described as "hale and hearty.") Finally, there is "holy," the last step in the progression and the goal of the journey.

At first glance, there is some irony in linking the second half of life with themes of healing and fertility. Even the inclusion of wholeness is questionable, since for some this stage is defined by a grave or terminal illness. As already noted, age is not necessarily a factor; typically, however, we associate the second half of life with arrival at a certain chronological age, somewhere around forty. Then, even for those in excellent health, inevitable physical results of aging begin to manifest themselves. I recall my moment of panic when I realized that I could no longer read the telephone book. I thought of Bette Davis in *Dark Victory*—I would be blind, even dead by sundown! When I sought out an ophthalmologist, he congratulated me on my remarkably healthy eyes and diagnosed my condition as presbyopia—*old vision.*

Of course our physical decline begins at birth, when the previously life-giving umbilicus becomes obsolete, withers, and falls off. It is downhill from there; if we live long enough, we can look forward to hair loss, wrinkles, thinning bones, osteoarthritis, an increasingly unreliable urinary system, hearing loss, cataracts, and what the experts call "benign senescent forgetfulness." If I dwell too long on these facts of life or if I spend too long looking in the mirror, I begin to wonder: Is my organ donor card still useful? Do I have anything anybody might want?

But before I get too gloomy, I remember my friend Ellen, who let me walk with her near the end of her long life. On one occasion I had been called to the hospital where she was gravely ill and not expected to live. At ninety-two she was resisting a feeding tube and had somehow managed to indicate that I was authorized to speak for her. We had talked often about death, or rather she had talked and I had listened, so I knew that she feared painful, invasive procedures at the end of her life. That night, when my negotiations with the hospital staff were over, I took her hand and promised her that there would be no drastic treatment without her consent. She had been semi-conscious and almost delirious; I was not sure that she understood what I had said. But then her eyes opened, sharp as ever, and she reached up to pat the hand of the young resident physician standing on the other side of the bed: "I want you to know, dear, that if I have anything you can use after I am gone, please feel free." He was speechless, and I knew that I could safely leave her. Later, when she had recovered, she remembered the almost mythic qualities of that night in the brightly-lit hospital room but denied her mischievous offer of *very* used body parts.

Gus was another friend who regarded his aging body with good-humored irony. He liked to chat about heaven and what he might expect there. He was at least twenty years younger than Ellen and in good health, so there was no frightened urgency in his speculations, just a kind of childlike curiosity. "I don't know about this body," he said. "I've lost my hair, and I take my teeth out at night. I can't see a thing without my glasses. And on top of all that, my chest has slipped." He looked down ruefully and patted his ample midsection. "I only hope I don't get this body back—I'd like to have an earlier version."

Gus and Ellen were whole people, even though Ellen lay near death and Gus's body was visibly deteriorating. Theirs was not the unblemished wholeness of the perfect newborn, but rather the worn wholeness that grows out of a lived life.

From Brokenness to Wholeness

Thirty years ago I lived in a rented house in Buenos Aires for a year. One of its chief attractions was a washing machine, which the owner displayed to me proudly. By my standards it was ancient and battered, a piece of junk, but I politely agreed with her that it was indeed a treasure. I kept it alive throughout my tenancy although it wheezed and groaned. Sometimes it broke down altogether; then the neighborhood handyman would come, his tools tied in a cloth bundle fastened to the handlebars of his bicycle. "Ah, senora," he would say, "what a beautiful machine!" To him, brokenness was a challenge to be addressed again and again. To him, my piece of junk was a beautiful machine: he could see something that was invisible to me.

Our inability to tolerate material brokenness inundates us with debris. Unique to our time and culture is the preoccupation with the cost of waste disposal, the phenomenon of automobile graveyards, and odysseys of barges towing garbage out to sea. As computers rapidly become obsolete, to be replaced by new and ever better models, I read that we face a crisis: what to do with the millions of tons and cubic feet of discarded and now worthless technology. On a homelier scale, here in Jenkins Hollow my neighbor's yard is decorated with two defunct cars and one dead truck with "Mabel" painted on the cab door. When his present battered station wagon succumbs, it will no doubt join Mabel and her nameless companions as monuments of brokenness beyond repair.

But we are not household appliances and automobiles; we are God's children. We know we were meant to be whole, and we have a deep memory of lost wholeness. We yearn for it. And we know—but perhaps deny—that we are broken. We are not toasters and tape players. Surely it is not too costly a process for us to become whole.

Before we can become whole, at whatever cost, we must recognize our brokenness as part of the human condition. We know that, inevitably, we will be wounded and damaged. This knowledge runs like a dark thread through our lives, apparent in even the most joyful moments. When the infant Jesus was presented in the temple, the aged Simeon recognized him as the Christ. This was surely a moment of joy for Mary. All mothers know that their children are remarkable, small witnesses to the wonder of incarnation. But for Mary, this was a public ratification of what she already knew, that this child was truly unlike any other. It was a moment of celebration and promise. But then Simeon tells her a hard truth: a sword will pierce through her own soul also.

Simeon's words reinforce the poignancy of the nativity: we know that this story will lead to the cross, just as we know when we look at beautifully whole but ordinary newborns that brokenness is in store for them. Perhaps that is why we are moved when we look at happy pictures of ourselves as infants. Is that sunny little girl entranced by the new swingset really me? Could I ever have been such a picture of total delight? And I know that is why I am moved when I see the happiness of parents with their firstborn. How can they know that a sword will inevitably pierce their own souls also?

So to be broken is to be human. At the center of our life together is a God who lets himself be broken, who speaks to us each time the eucharist is celebrated. But there is a paradox. While brokenness is a presupposition of our humanity and while God is with us in our brokenness, the whole message of the gospel is that we are intended to be whole. We are missing the point if we read the healing stories as accounts of medical cures of specific ailments—ah, this is how Jesus deals with a malfunctioning optic nerve; this is how he controls bleeding of unknown origin without recourse to surgery; this is how he rehabilitates the paralyzed. Christ's mission of healing is a mission of the restoration of wholeness. In other words, the healed become the people God intended them to be: intact, complete, and functioning. They are in harmony with themselves, with others, and with God.

It is tempting to read gospel accounts of healing as "happily-ever-after" stories: the story ends with the restoration of health and wholeness. It is easy to forget that healing can be difficult, frightening, and challenging. When the beggar Bartimaeus asked to receive his sight, did he know how much his blindness had protected him from pain and ugliness, how it had shielded him from really knowing the world around him? Being healed restored him to full participation and accountability in the human family.

First of all, of course, we must want to be healed. When Jesus encountered the man who had been ill for thirty-eight years lying beside the pool of Bethesda, he asked him, "Do you want to be healed?" This seems an absurd question: the man has somehow dragged himself to a place known for its curative powers and has been lying beside the healing waters for "a long time." He must want to be healed! But his response to Jesus reflects the confusion and doubt many of us feel about accepting wholeness: without answering Jesus directly, the lame man explains how he has been impeded—he has no one to help him, and other people always push ahead of him to get to the water. Jesus wastes no words: "Stand up, take your mat and walk" (John 5:9).

My friend Steve reminds me of the man lying beside the pool. He is the rector of a small parish, where he is chronically frustrated. He is a good and loving priest and his parishioners are good people; they are simply wrong for each other. So whenever I have lunch with Steve, I am prepared to hear the now-familiar litany of what is wrong in his parish, how thwarted he is at every turn, how much he would like to accomplish in his ministry—if only he had someone to help him and if only those heedless other people did not push and get in his way. "Get up and walk!" I want to say. But Steve has become accustomed to lying beside the pool and thinking about what he *would* do if conditions were optimum. I am not sure that he really wants to be healed.

The gospel writers don't reveal anything about the state-of-mind of Peter's mother-in-law, but they tell us that after her healing she got up and served Jesus and the household. Maybe she did it gladly, but restoration of her health meant a return to the humdrum of routine, to long hours of repetitive domestic labor. It is not easy to go back to the kitchen after being the center of attention, after being set apart even by a painful illness. No fireworks, no brass bands, no celebration—just put on your apron and get back to work! It may not be easy to see the gift of blessed ordinariness that comes with healing.

Sometimes it is hard for those around us to accept the fact of our healing. When Jesus violates the law of the sabbath by healing the man with the withered hand, onlookers in the synagogue are furious. That he has broken the rules disturbs them so much that they want to destroy him, and they are unable to rejoice in the restoration of wholeness. We are less concerned with such meticulous observance of the sabbath, but sometimes we are angered and distressed by healing that calls our structures and patterns of living into question. I know one woman, Louise, who had become very comfortable with her husband's alcoholism. Her willingness to "put up with it" had won her a reputation of sanctity in the small community, and she had developed "not complaining" into a fine art. When Sam came to himself and began to work actively toward his own healing, Louise's world fell apart; she surprised herself—and Sam—by the depth of her anger at him. She had defined herself by his unhealth. His healing broke all her rules.

Sometimes it is hard for the healed to go home again. I think about this when I read the story of the Gerasene demoniac in Mark's gospel. The herdsmen flee when the demons leave the sick man and enter the swine; when the townspeople see the demoniac "sitting there, clothed and in his right mind," they beg Jesus to leave the neighborhood. The healed man wants to go with him, but Jesus refuses: "Go home to your friends, and tell them how much the Lord has done for you, and what mercy he has shown you" (Mark 5:19). That can't have been an easy conversation, particularly if the swine's owner got there first to complain about his considerable property loss. Did the healed man have any friends to go home to? And were they able to believe in his healing and to accept his wholeness? Or was he forever set apart as someone existing on the margins of the community, having to prove again and again that he was indeed well?

Healing, after all, does not erase the slate. Out of our brokenness we can gain compassion and insight, and ugly scars and hurts can become the raw material for creating rich and beautiful texture. The people healed by Jesus did not go back and live their lives over, this time without blemish. Rather, their brokenness became the fruitful matrix for a new life of wholeness.

My friend Ellen's worn-out body could not be healed. To be sure, she could be helped toward temporary relief in a painful crisis and might recover briefly from her present illness. But, given her extreme age, she and I knew that death would come soon. She and I also knew that she was in need of healing. There were unhealed wounds in her life that needed to be brought to light, examined, and then let go. For decades she had struggled to be able to forgive her cold, abandoning mother. "I know I should forgive her," she would say. "I feel like a hypocrite every time I say the Our Father—forgive us our trespasses as we forgive those who trespass against us. That's hard to say and mean it. Sometimes it seems better just not to say it. It's a frightening prayer, if you stop to think about it. How can I expect to be forgiven if I can't forgive her, my own mother, after all this time?"

It was healing for Ellen just to tell the story of her addicted mother who used and abused her gifted daughter. She had worked with it in psychotherapy, and it had provided raw material for her poetry and fiction. But now, when death was imminent, it became new in the telling. Hidden bits were disclosed, and glaring omissions could no longer be glossed over. It was as if Ellen were uncovering and cleansing a hidden wound. Near the end, she began to dream of her mother in a new way, reassuring dreams of simply being together as two women. A lifelong New Yorker, Ellen chuckled as she told me about one, which she interpreted as a vision of heaven. "No green fields and pearly gates for me—no, a really great apartment building, the kind I could never afford to live in. Mother was there and she was so glad to see me! She told me the apartment next to hers was vacant, whenever I was ready to move in."

As hearers of the stories, we can be agents of healing. There is great relief in laying the burden down, even briefly, in the presence of a spiritual friend. And there is great relief in hearing that loving, trusted other acknowledge the reality of pain. Most of us have been schooled in the spirituality of the stiff upper lip. I learned the falseness of this stance years ago when I watched our Scottish pediatrician comfort my hurt and frightened child with a great, enveloping embrace and the words, "Och, poor wee thing!" The poor wee thing stopped crying at once, for she realized that another had understood her pain and did not seek to minimize it. I find myself still guided by the unquestioning, all-encompassing compassion of that kind man with a burr. While he cured with antibiotics, he brought healing just by being there.

The Barren Become Fruitful

According to the legend, Anne yearned in vain for a child until she was well advanced in years. Then, miraculously, she became the mother of Mary. Not surprisingly, in the Middle

Ages she became the patron of the barren—the unmarried girls who wished above all else to marry and bear children, as well as married women who were childless. Her name was also invoked by women in childbirth.

Anne's legend fits comfortably into scriptural tradition; it is a repetition of the familiar story of the matriarchs, our fore-mothers. It is a variation on the theme of barrenness over against the divine promise of fruitfulness. Sarah, the mother of Isaac; Rebekah and Rachel, the mothers of Jacob and Joseph; Hannah and Elizabeth, who bore the prophets Samuel and John the Baptist late in their lives—these are the women of our family history, our direct ancestors. We tend to neglect fruitful Hagar, like a not quite respectable relative; after all, she was a servant, and Ishmael turned out to be pretty wild. And Leah, Rachel's sister, bore children easily; but we are told that she had "weak eyes" and that Jacob didn't really want her in the first place. She, too, we put aside as periph-eral to the main story. In my childhood I felt that I knew all these women well, secondhand of course, in about the same way I knew the mothers and aunts and sisters from my mater-nal grandmother's stories.

These are stories about women who want children des-perately and who feel ashamed and deficient because of their childlessness. There is a quality of expectancy about them: it is vital that they bring forth new life. Without children, they are nothing. Their plight is accentuated by the presence of "lesser" women around them who bear children easily—slaves like Hagar, Bilhah, and Zilpah, or Leah, the unloved and unwanted wife. "Why," the barren women must have asked, "are they rewarded so undeservedly while we are denied what is rightfully ours?"

Human fertility is a powerful metaphor. I would in no way minimize either the almost numinous experience of birthgiv-ing or the suffering of those who yearn in vain for children. Some women choose not to give birth, and men can be fathers but not mothers. Hence for some of us, the imagery of childlessness is painful, and for others it seems irrelevant. It remains, however, a compelling evocation of spiritual barrenness.

In the fourteenth century, Meister Eckhart, the learned Dominican mystic whose personal life must have been far removed from the intimate concerns of human reproduction, preached compellingly of the birth of God in the soul. Again and again he drove home his point: we can all become pregnant with God. Conversely, man or woman, old or young, we can also share in the barrenness of Sarah and her sisters.

Barrenness is not synonymous with sterility. We welcome sterility in medical procedures: surgical operations and childbirth were doubly perilous before the need for antiseptic precautions was understood. But a sterile environment is one without life or even the possibility of life, without the benign bacteria as well as the deadly ones. A barren landscape is colorless, bleak, and dry; so, perhaps, is a barren person. Yet there is, albeit hidden, the potential for new life awaiting the right conditions for fertility—perhaps darkness, moisture, or enriching nutrients. Perhaps the acceptable time. Perhaps the gracious action of God.

Sarah, Elizabeth, and Anne all bore children in the second half of life. They were all too old for motherhood: the very thought was absurd. Not many people laugh in the stories of the patriarchs and matriarchs, but the account of Sarah's release from barrenness in the Genesis 17 and 18 is punctuated with laughter. When the LORD renames Sarai and calls her Sarah, promising that she will bear a son and "be a mother of nations," Abraham is convulsed. He falls on his face and laughs. Later, when the three strangers appear to him by the oaks of Mamre, they inquire after Sarah and then announce that she will bear a son before spring. Listening (eavesdropping?) behind the door of the tent, Sarah laughs to herself in disbelief. There follows a delightful little argument. The LORD asks Abraham why Sarah laughed, and she enters the conversation before her husband can reply for her. She denies that she laughed, "for she was afraid," but the LORD has the last word: "Oh yes, you did laugh" (18:15).

Yahweh has the last word, but his question remains unanswered. I wonder what he might have heard, had he deigned to speak to Sarah directly. Why did Sarah laugh? And how did Sarah laugh? What was the quality of this laughter? Was it bitter? Or perhaps a hearty belly laugh at the obtuseness of men? Perhaps it was the dismissive, self-deprecating laugh of a woman who considers herself unworthy of notice. Or might it have been the nervous laugh that covers fear, shame, and sadness?

I hope that Sarah laughed the robust laugh of freedom, which was also a laugh of joyous surprise. The writer of Genesis tells us that she was "advanced in age" and that "it had ceased to be with Sarah after the manner of women" (18:11). She had thought that it was all over and that the view on the other side of the hill was one of unrelieved bleakness. And to her surprise, she learns that the seeming end is a new beginning and that fruitfulness will come from her barrenness.

This period of life can be a time when we can let go of self as our perspective changes. Even if we need seventy or eighty years to accept our gift of freedom, we no longer have to feel responsible for the world, but can reorder and redefine all our priorities in matters great and small. (I have vowed that I will never again wear uncomfortable shoes, regardless of the elegance of the occasion, and that I do not have to read every page of every book I undertake. I can also say "I don't know" with previously unimagined ease.) We learn to nurture unforeseen kinds of new life, and we learn other ways of nurturing. Knowing that time is inexorable and change inevitable imparts a tinge of melancholy to this newfound freedom: when we know that no one is "too old" to bring forth new life, we are also almost painfully aware of its precious uniqueness.

Perhaps the second half of life—whenever it comes to us—is a kind of pause, a hiatus, when we are able to laugh with Sarah and look forward to the absurdity and wonder of unexpected new beginnings. Any time of seeming barrenness has not been wasteful; "empty" experience provides the necessary matrix for the new life to come. It can be a surprising time, when we learn that everything that has gone before—all the plodding, striving, and searching—is mere preparation. In the memorable last sentence of Philip Roth's novel *Portnoy's Complaint,* the psychotherapist Dr. Spielvogel, after he has endured thousands of hours—and hundreds of pages—of Portnoy's anguished ruminations, says to his patient, "So! Now ve begin!"

Some Hardships and Dangers

Periods of barrenness are never easy because we cannot know when or if they will turn into times of fruitfulness, and we do not live easily with open-endedness. When my first child was born, I read and reread Dr. Spock's chapter on "Unexplained Crying in the First Three Months" and found it cruelly ironic. In my fatigue and anxiety I thought, "He might as well be talking about three years or three decades. Three months is a long time, at least 2,160 hours; right now each hour is an eternity! And how can I trust him when he says that everything will sort itself out? I'm sure it will be like this for the rest of my life." Even as visible and audible evidence of my fruitfulness lay in her crib beside me, I was in a barren place!

We are not at our strongest in these unavoidable times of waiting when no clear resolution is in sight. At best, we can become anxious and discouraged; at worst, we become untrue to ourselves as despair leads to distorted perspectives and priorities. "The child"—whatever the fruit of our yearning and longing might be—becomes the object of idolatrous preoccupation.

Sarah, destined to be "a mother of nations," becomes cruel and destructive in her barrenness. In desperation she has offered her slave Hagar as a surrogate mother and then finds that envy grows within her like a caricature of Hagar's pregnancy. The author of Genesis does not flesh out the story with psychological speculation, but it is easy to picture the tense domestic triangle and Abraham's resignation when he tells his wife, "Your slave-girl is in your power; do to her as you please" (16:6). Sarah's treatment of Hagar is so harsh that the slave woman flees into the wilderness. An angelic messenger persuades her to return, but later Sarah banishes her because she cannot bear to see Isaac and Ishmael playing together. She says to Abraham, "Cast out this slave woman with her son; for the son of this slave woman shall not inherit along with my son Isaac" (21:10). Abraham is reluctant, but the LORD persuades him that Hagar and Ishmael will survive and prosper in exile. "Humor her," Yahweh seems to be saying. "We both know how difficult these old women can be."

This is a poignant story of one woman's cruelty to another. In her fear and jealousy, Sarah is unable to be generous, even to be just. She is unable to rejoice in the abundance of good in her own life because she is preoccupied with the good fortune of her rival. She is sure that she can be happy and complete only when the other is banished.

Sarah's sisters live on among us, and one of them sought me out not long ago. Jenny is in her mid-forties, married, with grown children. She has no economic worries, and her marriage is stable if not exciting; she has a moderately satisfying job as a librarian. People in her small community look to her a someone who "has it all," but she is feeling barren and ever more desperate. She senses that she is at a turning point in her life and has, for several years, been struggling to determine her next steps. For some time she has found support in Anita, who leads a small "spiritual friends" group in their parish. Initially, Anita was reluctant to assume this leadership, protesting lack of experience and special training. But as Anita has grown in self-confidence and gentle authority, Jenny's feelings toward her have turned bitter and selfish. When she came to see me, she was so filled with jealousy that the words came tumbling out: she was no longer heard or valued in the group; Anita deliberately minimized and humiliated her; "someone" should see to it that she was removed from leadership of the group. "Cast out this slave woman!" cries Sarah.

Fortunately, I knew Anita, so I avoided being caught up in Jenny's intense feelings even as I tried to listen to her story with compassion. Attentive but gently distanced, I was able to see what Jenny was not ready to accept. In her own time of aridity, as she yearned for new life, she could not accept Anita's fruitfulness. To be sure, at first she had appeared to rejoice in it, using Anita—like Hagar—as a surrogate. During this time, she was drawn to the prayer group and embraced Anita's leadership. But now she could not bear to see her sister move toward new life while she remained stuck and increasingly despairing. Jenny and Anita are sisters, even as Sarah and Hagar are sisters.

Jenny is at a critical turning-point. She is unable to see Anita move toward new life because she is unable to see Anita, only the dehumanized object of her envy. I cannot predict whether she will be able to let go of that envy as she lives out this time of barrenness in her own life. Right now, like Sarah, she is unable to see her own giftedness and to know that out of her own abundance she can afford to be generous. I am not Jenny's spiritual director; our relationship is informal and sporadic. I can refuse to join in her wish to "cast out" Anita. I can gently but persistently keep reminding her of her own gifts and potential for new life. I can keep her in my prayers. But that is all: this is Jenny's struggle.

Rachel's response to barrenness was also self-destructive and selfish, if not so cruel as Sarah's. Her unloved sister Leah, whose marriage to Jacob was the result of deception, bears four sons in rapid succession. Like Sarah, Rachel resorts to surrogate motherhood; like Sarah, she finds that she cannot live through others. It is not enough that she holds Bilhah on her knees while the servant woman gives birth. She must have her own child, and she cries out in desperation to her husband, "Give me children, or I shall die!" (Genesis 30:1).

Give me children, or I shall die! Rachel's whole identity, her whole being, is called into question by her barrenness. In her self-centeredness, her preoccupation with bearing a child has become an obsession. Her approach is aggressive; she attacks. Rachel's outcry suggests a useful diagnostic instrument, an easily administered, fill-in-the-blank test: Give me _____, or I shall die! The possibilities are myriad. I regularly encounter prospective seminarians for whom ordination is an obsession. After multiple rejections for admission to the process, they are unable to hear the wisdom of the community, unable to accept the judgment of screening committees, unable to let go of a fixed idea. What began as a sense of vocation has become idolatry. God's call has been drowned out or at least overlaid by a distracting and seductive voice: this thing I want—whatever it is—is of ultimate importance, and I must have it!

The object of desire is not necessarily bad; indeed, it may be wholesome, life-giving, and holy—at least initially. Marriage, the gift of children, an academic degree, and professional achievement are all potentially good. But when we find ourselves in a barren place, like Rachel, and raise our voices to cry, "Give me a husband, a child, a life partner, a promotion, a title, a degree—or I shall die!" we should know that we are in danger. We may achieve our wish by sheer exertion, and we do not die. But we will be spiritually deadened and probably disappointed in what we attain.

Carol fears living her life as a single woman more than anything else in the world. I met her first several years ago when she was seeking a spiritual director and had come to me for a referral. She was tall and attractive, with long brown hair and the lithe body of a dancer. When I asked her age—one of my routine questions—she bristled a bit and told me that she would rather not say. "Of course," I said. "No problem. It's just interesting how God gets our attention at different times in our lives and how certain ages are like thresholds. It's not important."

Our paths have crossed again over the years, and we have come to be friends of sorts. It was clear to me that Carol was lonely and that she wanted a partner, if not a husband. It was also clear that she dreaded growing old. One day she said, "You know, I ought to confess something." I braced myself. "Remember how, a long time ago, I didn't want to talk about my age? Well, I'm forty-seven." I wanted to say again that it wasn't important, but instead I waited for the rest of the story. She went on, "I really work hard at staying young. I have to. I haven't told you much about Rob, except that we're together. He's a lot younger than I am, a good ten years. I want to keep him. We have our ups and downs, but I think he wants to marry me."

In time, Carol told me about the "ups and downs." Rob has a violent temper and strikes her occasionally. "He's always sorry afterwards, almost like a little boy wanting to make up again," she said. Then too, Rob is jealous of her friends and contemptuous of her devotion to the church. Most telling for Carol, he is always conscious of the difference in their ages and misses no opportunity to point out telltale signs.

Carol is living out Rachel's cry, convinced that she cannot be a whole person without a husband—any husband, even a brutal one, is better than being alone. She is convinced that she cannot be a whole person in an aging body, that no one will love her if she stops looking young.

Taking Away the Reproach

For all these women, bearing a child is of utmost importance. In their barrenness, they are incomplete, not themselves; they feel guilt, shame, and sadness; they are misunderstood, minimized, and badly treated. Far from being a private concern, their condition is a matter of public interest and possibly ridicule. Hannah's story is especially poignant. Before Samuel's birth, she is distraught because she has no children. She weeps constantly and cannot eat. Her husband Elkanah treats her tenderly (in contrast to grouchy Jacob, whose "anger was kindled against" a similarly grieving Rachel). He asks, "Hannah, why do you weep? Why do you not eat? Why is your heart sad? Am I not more to you than ten sons?" (1 Samuel 1:8). Her answer is not recorded, but we can assume that it was a resounding "No!" or else continued weeping. When she prays in the temple, she is so agitated that the priest Eli reproaches her for public drunkenness. Her response is submissive, almost obsequious. "No, my lord," she tells him, "I am a woman deeply troubled; I have drunk neither wine nor strong drink, but I have been pouring out my soul before the LORD" (1:15). When she begs him not to think ill of her, it is as if she were apologizing for her own suffering.

There is no scriptural indication that their barrenness is a divinely ordained punishment, although the women may interpret their childlessness as a sign of God's disfavor. But it is clearly a reproach, a public shame and a public disgrace. The woman is not what she is supposed to be; something very basic is lacking. Sarah, Rachel, Hannah, and Elizabeth all perceive themselves as deficient. When Rachel finally gives birth to Joseph, she says, "God has taken away my reproach" (Genesis 30:23). In almost the same words, Elizabeth rejoices when she is pregnant with John the Baptist: "This is what the Lord has done for me when he looked favorably on me and took away the disgrace I have endured among my people" (Luke 1:25). On a literal level, these are stories of women living under patriarchy, women whose identity and worth were bound up in producing male heirs. Of course their barrenness was a reproach: in their culture they were failures.

The bearing of children is still a major preoccupation, a matter of primary concern to many prospective parents. Women—and men—who spend long years trying to conceive a child, subjecting themselves to elaborate diagnostic tests and treatments, must feel kinship with Rachel. We are witnessing the development of ever more sophisticated technology and the questionable use of surrogate mothers. Are the troubled birthgivers who renege on the contract perhaps the modern sisters of Hagar, Bilhah, and Zilpah, the slave women who conceived on behalf of their mistresses? But while there is ineffable sadness in infertility, in many parts of the world today a woman no longer needs to bear a child to complete or prove her identity. The reproach has been taken away.

While the childlessness of these biblical foremothers is no punishment, it is clear, however, that postponement of fertility is divinely ordained. The time of barrenness is a kind of preliminary, preparatory stage; its ending is often dramatic. The Annunciation is prefigured again and again. Sarah and Abraham are visited by angels; Rebekah becomes pregnant after Isaac prays on her behalf; God "remembers" Rachel, and she bears a son. Samson's unnamed mother is visited by an angel, who tells her, "Although you are barren, having borne no children, you shall conceive and bear a son." The angel goes on to outline a regimen of prenatal care: "Now be careful not to drink wine or strong drink, or to eat anything unclean" (Judges 13:3-4). Hannah receives no angelic messenger, but the LORD "remembers" her; when she presents her child in the temple, her exultant hymn of praise anticipates the Magnificat:

My heart exults in the LORD;
   my strength is exalted in my God.
My mouth derides my enemies,
   because I rejoice in my victory.
There is no Holy One like the LORD, no one besides you;
there is no Rock like our God. (1 Samuel 2:1-2)

These are not the words of a downtrodden failure, a groveling woman who begs an arrogant priest not to think badly of her!

Finally, like the completion of the progression begun with Sarah, the birth of John the Baptist is foretold when an angel appears to Zechariah: "Do not be afraid, Zechariah, for your prayer is heard. Your wife Elizabeth will bear you a son" (Luke 1:13). I wonder who told Elizabeth? At least Sarah was listening at the door of the tent!

We can see our barrenness, the arid and empty places where we seem to be stuck, as a reproach. God may not be angry, vengeful, or punitive, but is it possible that God might be forgetful? The psalmist seems to think so when he cries,

> Rouse yourself! Why do you sleep, O Lord?
>   Awake, do not cast us off forever!
> Why do you hide your face?
> Why do you forget our affliction
>   and oppression? (Psalm 44:23-24)

Scripture tells us that God "remembers" both Rachel and Hannah and that they are delivered from barrenness. God, infinite and all-knowing, cannot forget us. The God who keeps track of sparrows—and no doubt starlings and pigeons as well—must assuredly keep track of those made in God's image. God cannot not forget us, and God can indeed "re-member" us: put us back together again, restore us to wholeness.

New Life

What forms might our deliverance from barrenness take in the second half of life? What happens when God re-members us in maturity? What might that new life look like, the new life to which we have given birth?

New fruitfulness might simply mean going deeper. Like those healed by Jesus, we begin to see with new eyes and hear with new ears; for they too moved from barrenness to new life. To the casual observer there may be no outward change, as we go on doing the same things as before. But our perceptions are drastically altered, and we feel the need to move from life's surface to a new and mysterious place. This is the time when many people seek a spiritual director. They are restless and want something, and they know that it is not a material want. Whatever is at the bottom of that deep place is not a *thing*. God is *no thing*, Eckhart tells us. And the deep place in unfathomable; we will never get to the bottom of it.

My young friend Dave has always loved the outdoors and is thoroughly at home there. After a serious accident and an arduous period of recovery, he was able to return to his beloved mountains. They were the same, but he was different. His vision had changed—his inner vision (the accident had not harmed his eyes). Spiritually he now was gifted with presbyopia: his vision had become old. One October evening, as we stood together on a bridge over the noisy little Hazel River, he said, "You can hear God in that river. I used to get stuck on the idea of a God who was far away, scary, mad at me. Now I can't get over how much God loves me. And I can't get over how amazing everything is."

Dave is still young, but he has entered the second half of life. He looks much the same as he did two years ago, before he was so badly hurt: suffering, hardship, and his experience of God's grace have not marked him outwardly. He is a big, rugged man, a mountain man with a high school education. The God who re-membered him is not a God of intellectual abstraction, and Dave is quick to disclaim theological expertise—"I'm not a preacher or anything." But he has discovered a deep place within himself where the ordinary is transformed and sanctified and where the mystery is unfathomable.

Sometimes this surge of new life brings a vocational change. One place I see it is in the "graying of our seminaries," as people well into midlife feel called to turn their lives around. They don't often speak of conversion since the overwhelming majority have been faithful Christians for years, if not decades; but they have indeed experienced *metanoia*, conversion, a turning-around, a redirection of their lives. These are exciting people to be with. They are already richly textured, but they approach the newness in their lives with the intensity and zest of youth. And, of course, in one sense they *are* young: they have turned around and let themselves be renewed.

While these prospective deacons and priests are bringing both energy and wisdom to the church, it is important to reclaim the sense of vocation as relevant, indeed vital to *all* Christians. Those delivered from the dormancy of spiritual barrenness may experience a new commitment to ministry that has nothing to do with ordination. This may result in a change in secular employment, the abandonment of well-paid but spiritually deadening work for something riskier, humbler, and rich in promise. On the other hand, one's nine-to-five life may remain unchanged, but one's real life in Christ may be lived "in the cracks" and "after hours." Ministries of outreach flourish thanks to these often uncelebrated vocations. Feeding and shelter programs, ministry to the homebound aged, and much prison ministry depend on the faithfulness and enthusiasm of the laity, people who—to paraphrase my friend Dave—would say of themselves, "I'm not a minister or anything."

I met Henry only once, but it was a memorable meeting. A tall, rugged African American in his mid-fifties, he came driving down the dirt road before dawn on a December morning to take me to Culpeper to catch the 7 o'clock train to New York. A Yellow Cab in Jenkins Hollow is not a common sight! A cab ride in rural Virginia is a more intimate experience than a similar trip would be in Manhattan, so it was inevitable that we would pass the time chatting. Eventually, as we talked about work, Henry confided, "I had my own company for years. You'd be surprised how many folks need cabs, even out here in the country, and I was doing pretty good. But I gave it up three years ago because it was getting in the way of my real work. The Lord was calling me to work in his vineyard."

He went on to tell me that he had sold his cab and gone to work for his competitor, where his hours were more limited and where he could count on free Sundays. "I don't earn as much, but I earn enough. It doesn't take much if you're careful—and as old as I am." Henry's corner of God's vineyard was the prison farm and the county jail. "A lot of those guys don't have anybody. Most of them aren't really bad men, but they sure are messed up. I just go and talk to them. And listen to them, too—they aren't used to that. I don't preach; they aren't about to listen to a preacher. But it seems to make a difference, and I am pretty sure that's what God expects of me right now."

It was barely light as we approached the bleak little railroad station. Henry was relieved that others were waiting on the platform: "I wouldn't want to leave you standing there all alone." We shook hands and agreed to remember each other.

Last summer I needed to catch the 7 o'clock train again, so once again a Yellow Cab bumped down the dirt road in the early morning. It was a different driver. I asked about Henry and was told, "He hasn't worked for us for a while." Driving that cab, even for limited hours, must have been getting in the way of his real work.

In the second half of life we have the exciting prospect of coming to life for the first time. This raising to new life is not the same as Lazarus coming forth from his tomb with the odor of death clinging to him, but is rather a sudden and glorious awakening from dormancy. Sarah's experience tells us that it is never too late! This comforts me when I meet people who seem frozen, stuck, and joyless. There is always the possibility that they will some day say, "Shall I indeed bear a child now that I am old? Shall I indeed be fruitful and free?"

In our fruitfulness, we are able to live passionately. It is high time that we reclaim passion from advertisements for steamy romances and bad movies. When we live passionately, *everything matters.* Initially, that sounds alarming: if everything matters, won't we be overwhelmed and inundated? But if we are open and attentive to God (and to our own deepest self), we will remain proportionate. We will be like my friend Dave, sensitive and aware, but always clear about our priorities.

When I was growing up, we were required to memorize reams of poetry in school, and for me in my teens, Robert Browning was *the* poet. Some of his lines are embedded in my memory, particularly several from "My Last Duchess." As he negotiates for a new bride, the middle-aged duke proudly shows off the portrait of his recently dead young wife. It is clear that he regards her as a prized and beautiful, but ultimately disappointing, possession. What he describes as her "faults" are indications that she lived passionately: "She had a heart—how shall I say?—too soon made glad." Her priorities are incomprehensible to him—the gift of a branch of cherry blossoms, the sight of a sunset, even the white mule she rode around the terrace delighted her.

> ...She thanked men,—good! but thanked
> Somehow—I know not how—as if she ranked
> My gift of a nine-hundred-years-old name
>   With anybody's gift.

It is implicit in the poem that her passion, her gift of being open to everything around her, could not survive the coldness of her lord.

When we live passionately, we are not afraid to feel, to let our hearts be made glad, but we are also not afraid to feel our own pain and the world's. When we live passionately, we are open, even though openness can be dangerous to our complacency. When we live passionately, we take a page from the handbook of natural childbirth enthusiasts and resolve to bring forth new life without benefit of anesthesia.

In our fruitfulness, we also live generously. Re-membered by God, we have experienced his love, glimpsed his infinite mystery, and tasted of his generosity. I think of the heavenly banquet as a Dickensian Christmas feast, God's generosity a great banquet, and our own generosity the fruit of our gratitude. It is the generosity of trusting children, in which we invite others to share the bounty of the family table. I was always touched and honored when I would overhear my children assure visiting playmates that of course they could stay for dinner because there would be plenty. As trusting children we know too that *we* are not the host and provider.

To live passionately and generously is freedom. To live passionately and generously is delightful—to be filled with delight. Filled with delight and new life, we may still look like our ordinary and unglamourous selves. People might even laugh at us; it is one of the risks of harboring amazing new life, for as Sarah said, "Everyone who hears will laugh over me." Perhaps we can join in, transforming it to the robust laughter of freedom and joyous surprise.

Harvest Time

It was August when I left the city for a five-month stay in Jenkins Hollow. The vegetation was lush and dense, the days hot, and the thunderstorms dramatic. I was sharing the space with at least two-thirds of the 900,000 species of insects, many of whom seemed attracted to me personally. The night sky was often a spectacular show of falling stars. The harvest was just beginning: tomatoes and yellow squash in unbelievable quantities.

Since I arrived, the landscape has been changing daily. On warm days, the ladybird beetles—so named because they were sacred to Mary in the Middle Ages—are swarming. The porch screens are covered with their tiny dark orange and black-spotted bodies, and they manage to enter the house through minuscule openings. I, who am usually uneasy with bugs crawling on my person, feel a certain affection toward them. I pick them from my hair and sweatshirt and escort them to the door, suggesting that they find a more appropriate place to winter. Some crickets are living under the porch. Since they, unlike most of their insect kin, do not move about but stay firmly in one place with a kind of Benedictine stability, I have come to know them—they are not just any old crickets.

Now the vegetation is dying down. Bit by bit, we have moved from green lushness to brilliant color. In another few weeks, stark gray, brown, and black will predominate on the rocky hillsides. It has taken me a long time to see the beauty of bare trees. It has also taken me a long time to appreciate bareness—I can see farther, and I can see things that would have been invisible under the cover of vines and leaves. Old stone walls, unnoticed in the summer, now stand out. The contours of the land are clearer, and it is possible to trace the path of abandoned roads through the woods. There are still a few apples to be picked, but the harvest—which began with the first cutting of hay in May—is nearly over. For this year. In a few months, new life will come from the present bare bleakness.

For the folk of the Middle Ages, Anne was the patron saint of the harvest. Her feast day varied from place to place, since harvest times would obviously vary according to the climate of the area, but July 26 is her somewhat curtailed day in the 1979 Book of Common Prayer; unnamed, she shares it with the also unnamed Joachim in the feast of "The Parents of the Blessed Virgin Mary." But at the height of her popularity, she was a real and homely presence as crops were gathered in; and haycutters invoked "dear holy grandmother Anne."[1]

It is almost a cliché to say that the second half of life should be a time of harvest. This may at some point cease to be a meaningful image, for most of us urban and suburban folk are

---

1   Kleinschmidt, p. 427.

out of touch with the rituals of harvest time. In New York, every conceivable fresh fruit or vegetable is available all the time, and strawberries in midwinter are no longer the stuff of fairy tales. I needed to come back to Jenkins Hollow to be reminded of the rhythms of growth and harvest that I knew so well in childhood. When green beans were ripe, you ate green beans—and more green beans, to the point of surfeit. When all other fresh fruits and berries have passed their time, you fall back on the humble and reliable apple.

The rhythm of the harvest is like the rhythm of craftwork: a long period of care and waiting precedes fulfillment. A bountiful harvest demands considerable skill and a lot of hard work. In the parable of the sower, Jesus reminds us of the conditions for growth: the seeds must remain undisturbed in the ground, the soil must be sufficiently deep, and thorns must be kept cleared away.

It is hard to be patient and leave the seeds in the ground long enough for them to germinate and achieve optimum growth. Even if birds do not come and devour them, we are often tempted to pull them up and check on their progress. We manage to speed up so many things, but there is no spiritual equivalent of the microwave or supersonic travel. The seeds have to stay in the ground for a long time before we can anticipate their fruits. The harvest might begin in the second half of life, but it isn't over until the very end.

And the soil must be deep. I remember my surprise when I realized that the root system of a tree must mirror the visible trunk and leaves. We city folk often see roots as an unsightly problem—they break up sidewalks and intrude themselves into subterranean pipes. Beautiful trees are fine, but roots are a nuisance! To put down our roots and let them spread through the darkness is not exciting work. It can be tedious, and it can be laborious. While we can see and admire what is flourishing above ground, perhaps even prune it or support it with a trellis, we can't see what is happening in the dark matrix of our growth. It is easy to persuade ourselves that nothing is happening.

Finally, the thorns and briars must not be permitted to choke the new growth. My ongoing battles with the ailanthus trees have become for me a symbol for combatting sin, or at least for the protection of good growth. These trees move quickly into any cleared spot, grow with incredible rapidity, and manage—by twisting their trunks to catch the sun—to flourish almost everywhere. When I cut one down, I find next year that five new ones have sprouted from the stump. They propagate chiefly by rhizomes that spread under the ground, with new trees popping up far from their parents. I know that the ailanthus is part of creation and that it has its own peculiar beauty: it is sometimes called Tree of Heaven. But I know too that it chokes out other plants and so I feel called to do battle with it. I chop, saw, and hack; and sometimes I am lucky enough to unearth a rhizome and triumphantly pull a whole root system out of the ground.

My pleasure in the battle startles me a little since I like to think of myself as a peaceable person, but I assuage my guilt by telling myself that it is a parable for the battle with evil. And perhaps it is. The ailanthus is not a bad tree: its leaves are not poisonous, and it emits no noxious odors. Its wood is soft; it bears no edible fruit for humans or animals; in short, it is bland and undistinguished. Left unchecked, however, it impedes and obstructs other growth as it moves inexorably into every available space and then spreads out. I wonder what the spiritual equivalents of the ailanthus might be? What bland yet choking distractions creep into our lives and fill all the spaces?

We are the harvest, but we are also the harvesters. In the ninth chapter of Matthew, in a passage often read at the ordination of priests, we read:

When [Jesus] saw the crowds, he had compassion for them, because they were harassed and helpless, like sheep without a shepherd. Then he said to his disciples, "The harvest is plentiful, but the laborers are few; therefore ask the Lord of the harvest to send out laborers into his harvest." (Matthew 9:36-38)

There is a certain romantic charm in these words, until I remember my own limited experience as a harvester and recall my childhood self picking strawberries, squatting in the sun and balancing carefully between the sprawling plants. It was hot work; muscles got cramped, and tiny bugs flew into my eyes. Eating strawberries was a foretaste of heaven, but picking them was something else.

So when I read this passage and think of the real harvest laborers of our own time—not picturesque Flemish peasants in a Breughel painting or Millet's gleaners—I know that there is nothing charming or quaint about their occupation. As we search for metaphors for our life in the spirit, it is more attractive to think of ourselves as journeyers (although journeys have their own perils and discomforts) than to picture ourselves as migrant laborers, itinerant apple pickers, stoop labor. To work in the harvest is to work long hours, to get tired, to have hurt hands and aching muscles. To work in the harvest is to repeat the same action again, and again, and again. To work in the harvest is to work under pressure of time and weather. But to sign on as a harvest laborer in the fields of the Lord is also to be invited to partake of the bounty, to come to the feast.

Embracing Ambiguity

I used to love teaching first-semester German. Everything was sharply defined; answers were either right or wrong, and students' progress could be measured and expressed in percentages. But even after a few months, ambiguity began to creep in as we moved deeper into the mystery of language. We had to deal with shades of meaning and inexplicable idioms. Meanings became hard to pin down.

Most of us like to know where we are and what we are doing. If we are compelled to wait, we want to know when the period of waiting will end and what will be its outcome. Often our eyes are so fixed on that outcome that we forget that we are living *now,* that the past is irretrievable and the future has not yet come.

Marge and I were young mothers together. As close neighbors, we talked chiefly about our children. Marge was always waiting for the next developmental stage, which promised to be better—when Mike just sleeps through the night, gets out of diapers, starts to kindergarten, learns to read, and on and on. For her, the present was to be endured, indeed to be noticed as little as possible, in the hope that someday her life would be tidy and manageable. We have lost track of each other, but I strongly suspect that "real life" is still just a little bit down the road for Marge—when her husband retires, when they move to a better climate, when Mike finally provides them with a grandchild, when somehow at last perfection is achieved.

In the wholeness of the second half of life, whenever it comes to us, we discover the marvelous freedom of living deliberately, yet *carelessly.* In the words of T. S. Eliot's poem "Ash Wednesday," we have learned "to care and not to care....to sit still, even amid these rocks." We have accepted what the old Celtic Christians called "green martyrdom." Red martyrs died for their faith, while white martyrs entered the way of pilgrimage, wandering, and exile. Green martyrs, on the other hand, knew the heroism and the sanctity of faithfulness to the ordinary. Green martyrs understood the discipline of the craftsman and the patience of the harvester. What a delightful coincidence it is that, according to tradition, green is Anne's color.

Chapter Five

A Good Death

Santa Anna, buena muerte y poca cama.
   (Saint Anne, good death, little [time suffering and
   lingering in] bed.   *— a seventeenth-century prayer*

From lightning and tempest; from earthquake, fire, and
flood; from plague, pestilence, and famine,
   Good Lord, deliver us.
From all oppression, conspiracy, and rebellion; from violence, battle, and murder; and from dying suddenly and
unprepared, *Good Lord, deliver us. — the Great Litany*

A few years ago, on Ash Wednesday, I stopped at the Korean green-grocers a short block from my office. As the clerk weighed and bagged my purchases, she pointed to my ash-marked forehead and carefully enunciated, "What is it?" She is a tiny, friendly woman; we have known one another for years and always exchange warm greetings, but language difficulties have kept us from deep conversation. Her curiosity must have got the better of her after several hours of observing the seminary population and our Roman Catholic neighbors, all with apparently dirty faces.

I struggled to find the words. I wanted to take her question seriously, but I also knew that she needed neither a sermon nor a lecture. Finally I said, "It means that we're all going to die." As she began to commiserate with me, I hastened to assure her that our death was probably not imminent and that the ashes were a symbol of something that comes to everyone.

Our death is inevitable, but everything we "know" about it is theoretical or secondhand. We can read books and attend lectures, be present at the death of others, and experience the inescapable losses that come with the years. Certainly, if we live long enough, we have inevitably practiced for our death in myriad little ways. Merely living is like involuntary participation in a spiritual Lamaze class, preparing us for the final great passage. But just as a Lamaze class—however valuable—is no substitute for the reality of giving birth, so too we cannot anticipate the experience of death. We cannot place ourselves within it or know how we will act and react.

Most of the time I am able to ignore my intuitive flashes of my own impending death, but at odd times I am suffused with an acute awareness. This is rarely grim; sometimes it is even humorous. Eager to end my work day, I might be impatient at the slow arrival of the train. As I pace the subway platform and watch for the light down the tunnel, I hear an inner voice—not scolding, not frightening, merely matter-of-fact—"What are you fussing about? Slow down. Take what comes. Live this moment. You'll be dead before too long." I can hardly classify this as a mystical experience, but it certainly is a salutary one, restoring me to right proportions and reminding me good-humoredly of my insignificant place in God's scheme of time. I am reminded yet again that the present moment is all that I have.

If we cannot know our deaths, we are nevertheless inescapably aware of our mortality. We live with our own small reminders, our own "last things." We are not commonly reminded of our mortality by reflecting on heaven, hell, death, and judgment, but rather by our usually fleeting awareness that our lives are not static, that we are not the same people in the same place that we were ten years ago. Or for that matter, ten days ago.

I realized this when I was briefly reunited with the best friend of my student days. We had backpacked in Europe years before such travel became almost a rite of passage for middle-class American youth. We had stayed awake many nights discussing cosmic questions: poetry, boyfriends, our parents, our past, our future, God. When we met again as grandmothers, my first reaction was, "She's *matronly!* Is this the pal who could dance all night? Is this my companion of third-class Spanish rail travel?" I suspect that similar thoughts coursed through Ardyth's mind in those first seconds before we recognized the old friend and recovered the intimacy of a shared past. Seeing her, however, helped me to see myself; like a mirror she enabled me to mark my wear and tear, changes and growth, not just in outward appearance, but in my inner self.

The inexorable changes of living are always accompanied by loss, even if we do not recognize it at the time. All the incidents of "lastness" are little rehearsals for our death; were we to notice them, we would become *too* aware, *too* self-conscious. We would observe life rather than live.

Every now and then I look at my nearly middle-aged children and ponder: why didn't I notice when I changed the last diaper? Why didn't I pay attention and celebrate—or mourn—all the last things? There was the last time of dozing uneasily on the living room sofa, listening for a car and hoping that my adolescent would come home safe and sound before the curfew. The last report card, opened with apprehension—would the family poet survive algebra? As I reach farther back in my life, there was the last banana split—Katz's drug store, July 1947. The last bicycle ride—probably sometime in the late 1960s, unless I miraculously regain lost agility.

The preciousness of the ordinary can often be grasped only in retrospect. This no doubt explains the ongoing popularity of *Our Town*, a sentimental and not very good play that nevertheless brings people to tears, even in clumsy amateur performances. Thornton Wilder was on to something. He understood finality, the little "last things" that punctuate our lives, that remind us of our transience.

I can close my eyes and remember the smell and feel of my children as babies, even though I have no desire to return to those days of full-time mothering nor for three satisfactory adults to revert to infantile helplessness. But every now and then, like Emily in Our Town, I would like to go back for just a little while and reassure myself that nothing is changed or lost. As I write, summer has given way to autumn, and now autumn is turning into winter. The neighbor down the road, whom I rarely saw but who always greeted me with two jaunty taps on the horn as he drove by, doesn't come by anymore. He is dying. He has moved into town, where family can care for him.

I am living in solitude in a creaky old house. My desk is the old kitchen door, removed when we knocked out a wall fifteen years ago and now propped up on two sawhorses. I am aware of all the people who have been born in this house, quarrelled in it, loved in it, eaten in it, died in it. I catch myself wondering who will sit next by my workroom window to watch the river and the road and the line of trees on the skyline. Will my desk become a door again, or will it be firewood? My melancholy at first took me by surprise, but there is a *rightness* about it. For a little while, I have stopped holding awareness of my mortality at bay; I have invited it to come in and make itself at home.

Numbering Our Days

The little prayer at the beginning of this chapter comes from seventeenth-century Spain, where devotion to Anne flourished. The devout prayed to her in the hope that she would send them a "good death." Of course, death was always near at hand and it was impossible to hide from its terrors. The coming of death was inevitable—the big questions were "When?" and "How?" The possible "bad" deaths are catalogued in the Great Litany—lightning, tempest, earthquake, fire, flood, plague, pestilence, famine, violence, battle, and murder. And from dying suddenly and unprepared, good Lord, deliver us. Those big questions are still with us, even though most of us no longer think in terms of good and bad death: our culture tells us that all death is bad, and we learn early to regard it as a dirty secret. It can be no surprise that the idea of preparing for death consciously and cheerfully now seems quaint and anachronistic.

One of the fruits of my browsing at the annual book sale of the local historical society is a fragile, water-stained Book of Common Prayer, published in Philadelphia in 1856. It is a beautiful old book, complete with the Psalter and texts of two hundred rather austere hymns, only a few of them still current in our worship. It is a mysterious old book too, for there is no name—either of individual or parish—inscribed in the cover, and I find myself wondering what sorts and conditions of men and women might have read and cherished it before it found its way into the damp basement of the Rappahannock Historical Society. One of its treasures is the form for family evening prayer:

> The Family being together, a little before bed time, let the Master or Mistress, or any other whom they shall think proper, say as follows, all kneeling....

Then follows the Our Father, intercessions, and thanksgivings, and the prayer for God's protection during the night, including this straightforward reminder of death's inevitability:

> Make us ever mindful of the time when we shall lie down in the dust; and grant us grace always to live in such a

state, that we may never be afraid to die; so that, living and dying, we may be thine....

I try to imagine what it must have been like, to grow up with that prayer implanted in one's very marrow from the earliest days of consciousness!

We save money for retirement, we strive for maximum insurance coverage, and we draw up living wills to ensure that we will be spared invasive medical treatment or painful prolongation of life. Ironically, most of us would recoil at the idea of actively, cheerfully preparing for a good death as a part of daily family routine. And what is a good death, anyhow? Surely it is more than the cessation of physical life with minimum pain.

Even as we pray for deliverance from all the "wrong" deaths of the litany, we know that we are mortal. We know that we are transients—"For I am but a sojourner with you, a wayfarer, as all my forebears were" (Psalm 39:14)—and we know too that, at some point, death will be our inevitable next step on the journey. The Psalms are filled with reminders of our fragile hold on earthly life, contrasting our fleeting presence with Yahweh's unchanging timelessness:

You turn us back to the dust and say,
  "Go back, O child of earth."
For a thousand ages in your sight are like
    yesterday when it is past
  and like a watch in the night.
You sweep us away like a dream;
  we fade away suddenly like the grass. (Psalm 90:3-5)

I have written of my friend Ellen, who let me walk a few steps with her as she moved toward death. Childless and widowed, she died without close family. She had wished to be cremated—to return to the dust—but had made no plans for the disposition of that meager residue of ash. Her parish church had a columbarium, which she rejected. "I don't want to feel closed in," she said. "Those little niches are like post office boxes; that's no place to spend eternity."

To the relief of her executor, I volunteered to take possession of the ashes, referred to as "cremains" on the certificate of cremation. (I did not know whether to laugh, cry, or cringe at the neologism. What, I wondered, would the psalmist do with *that?*) On a clear winter day I climbed the hill behind the house in Jenkins Hollow, carrying the box of ashes, my prayer book, and a trowel. I had already chosen the spot—a grassy little ledge at the foot of a great rock outcropping. It was a favorite place to sit, leaning against the huge gray rock and looking across the valley at the mountains of the Blue Ridge.

It was easy to dig a hole, but then I wondered what to do next. Something made me recoil from burying the cardboard box; it felt like disposal rather than committal. So I opened the box and found the ashes were sealed in a sturdy plastic bag. It seemed right to me for Ellen's ashes to return to the earth, for her particles to mingle directly with the particles of loamy soil, so I poured the contents of the bag into the hole and patted a covering of earth over it. Then I read the eighty-fourth psalm, which had been one of her favorites.

> How dear to me is your dwelling, O LORD of hosts!
> My soul has a desire and longing
>   for the courts of the LORD;
> my heart and my flesh rejoice in the living God.

It is a song of journey, homecoming, and security. To be sure, we are transients, and my friend Ellen had gone from my life if not from my memory. But the grayish, slightly gritty ash, which would soon be indistinguishable from the soil around it, was not the last word. It spoke of her mortality, *was* her mortality, but it was not the last word.

When I worked as a chaplain in a residence for the frail aged, Ash Wednesday was a major liturgical event. At first this puzzled me, especially when I realized that some residents managed to attend two services: they would receive ashes from the Roman Catholic chaplain and then return a few hours later for the Episcopal rite. The bedridden would send messages to the chapel: be sure I get my ashes! It made me uneasy to stand before a wheelchair or bend over a bed, to mark a cross on a lined forehead, already almost skeletal, and intone, "Remember that you are dust, and to dust you shall return." It seemed like more truth than was really needed at the moment. So I was doubly surprised to hear the response, "Thank you, dear."

I learned something about human fragility and transience from these very old people among whom I ministered: we are dust, we shall return to dust, and it is all right. Far from being frightened or depressed by the tangible reminder of their mortality, they were comforted by it. The words of the Ash Wednesday rite were a promise rather than a threat: they promise a homecoming, a return. They recall the story of creation:

> Then the LORD God formed man from the dust of the ground, and breathed into his nostrils the breath of life; and the man became a living being. (Genesis 2:7)

I was reminded of the nursing home residents and their toughness in the face of frailty when I attended an Ash Wednesday liturgy at a determinedly upbeat parish. While my frail and impaired friends had looked willingly into the abyss, the starkness of the rite was softened for this congregation. As the priest signed each person with ashes, he said, "Turn aside, and receive the good news." I wanted to shout, "That's not the same thing at all! Why not throw away the ashes and hand each one a daffodil?" It is hard to see the good news in the ashes. Most of us would rather not number our days.

Our grandparents died at home in their beds; now it is rare to die in familiar surroundings and in the presence of loved ones. In the hospital where I worked for several years, no one ever died—they "ceased to breathe." So the code calling the chaplain for the commendatory prayers was "CB," and after a busy night one might hear the complaint, "Three CBs! I hardly got any sleep." Other hospitals have their own circumlocutions, but the basic picture is the same: when death is imminent, we are consigned to the care of strangers. "Doing everything possible" for the patient may have little to do with attention to physical or spiritual comfort; indeed, aggressive care is often invasive and painful, death itself a lonely experience.

When my older daughter was about four, she woke in the night with an earache. (For those too old to remember, an earache is a wicked pain.) I gave her an aspirin, supplied a hot water bottle, and said, "Elizabeth, there's nothing else I can do until morning. Then we'll talk to the doctor and get an antibiotic." She accepted the painful reality, but asked, "Is it all right if I just cry softly?" I almost cried myself then and asked if it would help if I lay beside her and held her. I did, and she soon fell asleep.

That incident has stayed in my mind. It taught me about the tenderness that children—maybe all of us—need, and about our ultimate helplessness against pain. Most important, though, it taught me something about the power of presence. I eased my daughter's pain simply by being there, by assuring her that I would not leave her, and by acknowledging the fact of her suffering. Why, I wonder, can we not do this for the dying? Why do we not have time merely to *sit* with another, doing nothing except perhaps holding a hand? This is spiritual work, not medical treatment or mental health care.

Holy Dying

For Christians, while death is inevitable, it is familiar—in the truest sense of the word—and can be befriended. Believers who prayed to Anne for a good death knew this. In his great hymn of praise, *The Canticle of the Sun,* Francis of Assisi reminds us of our kinship with all creation. Sun, wind, and fire are our brothers; moon, water, and mother earth are our sisters. And death, too, is our sister:

> Be praised, my Lord, for our sister,
>   the death of the body,
> from which no one living is able to flee.

How can we get ready for our sister's embrace?

In the past fifty years, preparation for childbirth has become commonplace. Prospective parents read books and attend classes. The mother makes herself ready, almost like an athlete in training, with attention to diet and exercise. Alcohol, caffeine, and nicotine are banished. There is practice for the birth itself even though the profound reality of birthgiving cannot be captured in anticipation.

I sometimes think of this on airplanes, when for the umpteenth time I obediently follow the flight attendant's instructions about "emergency procedures," locate the nearest exit, and gaze trustfully at the place overhead from which the oxygen mask will drop if needed. I let myself wonder for a moment if my seat cushion will indeed transform itself into a "flotation device" and how it might feel to exit—to what?—by one of those slides which, I am promised, will appear as if by magic. I usually abandon my fantasies before they become too vivid, aware that the preparatory drill is of vital importance but that no amount of instruction can duplicate the *real thing*. Some surprise—whether we are anticipating birth or an airline disaster—is an inevitable part of the program.

Surprise is an inevitable part of death, as well. Earlier times were more comfortable with intentional preparation for death, indeed went about it in ways that bear striking similarities to childbirth training in our own time. One such practical, down-to-earth, and compassionate manual on the good death is Jeremy Taylor's *Holy Dying.*[1] When I first picked it up, moti-

---

1   Jeremy Taylor, *Holy Dying* (Oxford: Clarendon Press, 1989).

vated by an urge toward scholarly thoroughness, I expected a dry and dated treatise. Instead, I found myself listening to the voice of a wise friend, someone who knew life—and death—firsthand.

Writing in the mid-seventeenth century, a time of instability when Sister Death was a constant companion, Jeremy Taylor offers us a book of spiritual direction on the art of dying well. In the dedication he emphasizes that we should begin early to practice for our death, that life itself is a preparation for its end. Dying well, he says, is a great art and a lifelong work. When we finally die, we are simply putting into practice what we already know. His main point, stressed again and again, is this: the skills for dying well must be learned by the healthy and vigorous. He does not use the word, but he is writing eloquently of the *crafting* of one's death.

Our squeamish age is probably not strong enough for his catalog of the natural signs of mortality. His vision has no place for the Tooth Fairy, that bringer of gifts to celebrate a new level of maturation. Instead, even the loss of baby teeth is an occasion of *memento mori*—"At the end of seven years, our teeth fall and dye before us, representing a formal prologue to the Tragedie." And a receding hairline is more than a blow to male vanity; "Baldnesse," he tells us, "is but a dressing to our funerals, the proper ornament of mourning...."

I have not yet recommended *Holy Dying* to those who seek spiritual direction with me, nor would I regard it as a suitable gift for the typical convalescent or confirmand. But there is great truth and wisdom in it, once one gets past its linguistic quaintness and its occasional excesses. For example, I find it difficult to subscribe to the idea that the person who "would die well must always look for death, every day knocking at the gates of the grave." Awareness of mortality is well and good, but such intense preoccupation would perforce impede our living. Taylor's insistence on self-knowledge, however, is neither death-obsessed nor life-impeding. He urges a daily *ex-*

amen of conscience—"He that does not frequently search his conscience [is] a house without a window"—and shows great awareness of our propensity for sin. These are not the grandiose sins that are the stuff of high drama, but the very ordinary shabby sins which most of us can recognize. We misuse time and language; we are vain and hypocritical; and, most important, we are skilled in self-deception. We daily abuse our God-given liberty; when we are brave enough to pay attention, we notice "our little greedinesses in eating, our surprises in the proportions of our drinking, our too great freedoms and fondnesses in lawfull loves."

The archaic spelling may render Taylor's catalog quaint, but some things haven't changed much in three and a half centuries. The human creature remains devious and self-deceptive, sliding easily into that gray area that blurs "the niceties of difference between some vertues and some vices, the secret undiscernible passages from lawfull to unlawfull." We need to keep an eye on ourselves, and we need the help of loved and trusted others to do so. Otherwise, to use Taylor's words, it is all too easy to remain "in love with small sins."

Part of his counsel is addressed to the sick, but I find it to be sound spiritual direction for all of us moving toward a good death. Taylor urges patience, which—when we pick the word apart—is related to both passion and passivity. The patient is one who suffers. The patient is one who is powerless in the face of affliction, who must at some point be passive, let himself be *done unto.* In a sense, merely by living we are all patients, even at our most robust and lively. Surprisingly, Taylor is not a proponent of the stiff upper lip. Suffering in silence may make life easier for those around us but does not always benefit the sufferer: "Therefore, silence and still composures, and not complaining, are no parts of a sick mans duty; they are not necessary parts of patience."

It has taken years for my friend Monica to be able to admit that she hates the progressively degenerative disease that will ultimately take her life. For a long time, she struggled with the idea that it was a test, even a kind of perverse gift from a loving father God. "He must love me a lot to have sent this to me," she used to say. Repeatedly, I pointed out that most earthly parents, however imperfect, wish health and wholeness for their children and that only the most depraved would willingly condemn them to a life of suffering. I have no easy explanation of why she, and not someone else, is stricken. For that matter, I—and generations of theologians wiser than I—have no cogent rationale for human sickness, pain, and degradation. But I am convinced that God, as manifest to us in the Incarnation, can be our partner in suffering. The one who died on the cross knew and knows about pain—not just cosmic "spiritual" pain, but also the humiliating, overwhelming pain of a broken body. The incarnate and crucified God can, I am sure, receive and understand our complaints.

The danger, of course, is getting stuck in our distress. Even as we can fall in love with our small sins, we can fall in love with our misery. What begins as an honest acknowledgment of pain and a healthy expression of anger can swell to enormous proportions and engulf us. This is surrender to despair; true patience, however, must be without despair. In other words, we dare not relinquish hope, which would mean giving our adversity ultimate power over us. Yet hope is fragile and elusive—"a thing with feathers," Emily Dickinson tells us.[2] Hope very often does not make sense; for, perching in the soul, it "sings the tune without the words." Most of us want to know the words, finding a tenuous security in their apparent precision and logic. But as Paul tells us in his letter to the Romans:

---

2   "Hope is a thing with feathers / That perches in the soul / And sings the tune without the words / And never stops at all." *The Complete Poems of Emily Dickinson,* ed. Thomas H. Johnson (London: Faber and Faber, 1970), p. 116.

Now hope that is seen is not hope. For who hopes for what is seen? But if we hope for what we do not see, we wait for it with patience. (Romans 8:24-25)

This past summer I lost a dear friend, a brother priest. As his death approached, he asked me to preach at his funeral. It was a conversation I shall never forget. David could no longer speak and had become so weak that writing was an effort; we both knew it was probably our last time together. Death, I think, was no longer terrible for him but had become the gentle sister of Francis's canticle. His comfort in speaking of her made me comfortable as well. When I asked him what Scripture he would like, he wrote, "I will take you to myself." Then he added, "From John's gospel."

I realized that this was part of the familiar passage beginning, "Let not your hearts be troubled." In choosing a few words from the heart of it, David helped me to look at it with new eyes. Unknowingly, he had given me a great gift in drawing my heart and mind to the promise contained in those six little words. That promise is part of the bed stone: it is the core of our faith. If we can believe in this promise, trust in it, nothing else matters much, even when the external circumstances of our lives matter terribly.

These six words are so simple. There are no conditions, qualifiers, or exceptions. The promise is straightforward, intimate, and filled with love: "Don't be afraid; I haven't forgotten you; I will come back for you; I will take you to myself; you are mine." This is the kind of promise mothers and fathers make to their children, the kind of promise that good parents know is sacred, inviolable.

In the days before David's death, as I carried these six words of Christ's promise with me, I found myself recalling a prayer of my earliest childhood:

If I should die before I wake,
I pray thee, Lord, my soul to take.

When my children were small, I heard that this was a "bad" prayer, one to be avoided because the linking of death and sleep might be frightening. What a pity! It is a prayer of hope, not fear; it is a prayer of sureness and safety. It should be our prayer. We should live it, even if we are too grown-up and sophisticated to add it to our daily devotions. We should live in the joy and hope of Christ's promise that, when he has prepared a place for us, he will come and take us to himself.

I somehow managed to preach that sermon without weeping. High in the pulpit, I looked down on David's bier and thought, "You have given me a gift. Now this is my gift to you—I'll try to pass your gift on to everybody in this big church, try to let them glimpse what you saw so clearly in your last days." I still have the dog-eared scrap of paper with David's last words to me.

Loss and Diminishment

I love the story in the last verses of John's gospel in which Jesus appears at dawn to the disciples, who have been fishing all night, and serves them breakfast on the beach. After they have eaten, he asks Peter not once, but three times: "Do you love me?" And each time Peter replies: "Of course!" And three times Jesus commands Peter to minister in his name: "Feed my lambs, tend my sheep, feed my sheep."

For years whenever I read this passage, I stopped before the end. There is such balance and symmetry in it: the question, the protestation of love, and the command to loving service, all repeated three times. There is drama, tension, and forgiveness, too, with each repetition of the question, "Do you love me?" and Peter's chance to redeem his three denials of Jesus. But the story doesn't end there. What follows is a reminder of the inevitability of loss:

> Very truly, I tell you, when you were younger, you used to
> fasten your own belt and to go wherever you wished. But

when you grow old, you will stretch out your hands, and someone else will fasten a belt around you and take you where you do not wish to go. (John 21:18)

This is the loss that is a part of martyrdom, whether ours is the witness of "red" martyrs who face the fierce wild beast or the more ordinary, even humdrum faithfulness of "green" martyrs who simply go on putting one foot in front of the other. It is a reminder that at some point we will very likely return to the helplessness and impotence of infancy: someone else will dress us and carry us where we do not wish to go.

I don't want to go there. I don't look forward to stretching out my hands in submission to that anonymous "other" or to giving up my autonomy, which (I think) I can disguise as faithful docility. And so I wonder: how will I behave when—*when* is more likely than *if*—I am helpless, dependent on others for my most rudimentary comfort and care? Will I become like Adelheid, so querulous that the most dedicated Meals-on-Wheels volunteer refused to enter her apartment? Or like Josephine, whose refusal to accept even the tiniest pleasure eventually drove away all visitors? To be dressed by another and taken "where we do not wish to go" is hard because we will not always be dependent on people whom we love and who love us. Care may be minimal, impersonal, or grudging.

I used to visit Grace, who was very old and confined to a wheelchair. She had been an independent woman in the early days when most of her sisters did not venture far from traditional roles: she had traveled the globe, achieved some success in the theater, and enjoyed a mild flouting of convention. Now, in her illness and immobility, she was dependent on her "home health attendants" for every intimate detail of her care and comfort. These were women supplied through an agency, minimally educated and poorly paid. Most of them disliked, even hated, their work, which they accepted because it was the only work they could obtain. Both they and

Grace felt trapped and angry for twelve hours each day in her tiny apartment.

Grace would never have claimed to be a patient woman. Her mind was quick, indeed seemed to become quicker as her body slowed down. She resented the indignity and loss of privacy that had become her daily life; what she hated and feared most of all, however, was her own descent into irritability and bad temper. With tears in her eyes and her voice breaking, she would tell me about losing her temper with "the girl": "I shouted at her. I have never shouted at anybody, but I shouted at her. And now I am sorry and ashamed of myself." A little careful questioning made it clear that Grace had not lost her temper without provocation and that the current attendant was rude and condescending. To her, Grace was clearly just another old lady who couldn't get herself to the bathroom. Another old lady who complained that the television was too loud. Another old lady who talked with big words and looked down on her.

Somehow that immediate situation was patched up. Grace insisted on apologizing for her loss of temper, an act of contrition which must have cost this proud woman dearly. The attendant seemed to try a little harder to understand Grace, then eventually moved on, to be replaced by a warm-hearted woman who liked old people. But the incident has stayed in my mind, chiefly because Grace was able to remain self-aware in her physical helplessness. She could see the danger of becoming a different person, querulous and unlovable. She was not concerned with justice: of course her caregiver *ought* to be sensitive and patient, *ought* to take Grace's age and disability into consideration, *ought* to meet her more than halfway. Grace knew that she could not change the attendant, nor could she change the external circumstances of her life. But she knew that she, however impatient and demanding of herself and others, could still be true to herself, even as she was carried where she did not wish to go.

I do not want to make this sound easy—it is not! Nor am I proposing that we cultivate behaviors and responses simply to elicit the desired behaviors and responses in others. The cultivation of patience may lead to some practical benefits, but that is not really the point. Power was not equally balanced between Grace and her attendant. Grace had greater inner resources, and she could use words with skill and accuracy. But her paid caregiver held very real physical power over the frail old woman. The caregiver also had the power to shame and mock her, and she knew—and Grace knew—that, at the very least, she was essential to Grace for the ordinary tasks of daily living. Grace's striving for true patience was a move toward her own inner freedom, her choice of a way to *be* when she no longer had choice of movement and action.

The second half of life, and most particularly the approach of death, brings a narrowing of the circle, a falling away of the extraneous. We should not be surprised when we are stripped of our treasures and possessions; as sojourners and wayfarers, we have not been promised permanence. The psalmist, after all, likens the LORD to a moth that "eat[s] away all that is dear to us" (Psalm 39:12).

When I worked among the frail aged, I was reminded again and again of the inexorable process of loss. With loss of mobility came a drastically restricted physical environment. Inability to negotiate the narrow stairs in her tenement made Irma a prisoner in her tiny apartment; then inability to move around even that small space brought her to a bed in half a room in a nursing home. Her world had literally become only a few square feet. She had quite literally been carried where she did not wish to go.

Similarly, Klara, a cultivated Viennese woman—I could still glimpse her elegance, even in the gray surroundings of the institution—never returned to her apartment after breaking her hip. She was moved directly to a nursing home where there was no space for her library. She thought about each of her books and mourned them as one might mourn lost children. The Readers' Digest series of condensed bestsellers, which was the chief staple of the home's collection, seemed to her a mockery.

Stories of loss are most poignant and irreversible when we let ourselves be open to the very frail aged or the terminally ill. Perhaps this is why these two segments of our population are often placed carefully out of our sight. For all of us, regardless of our relative youth and vigor, they can serve as icons, mirrors, and teachers. If we let ourselves be open to them, we can learn some of the facts of life—and of mortality.

We can learn about the narrowing circle. While Irma's world got physically smaller, there are other, equally painful ways in which our world can shrink. One of the most profound losses that we busy North Americans face is the absence of meaningful, creative, constructive work. This may be coincident with retirement from paid employment, but it is important to remember that meaningful work can continue long after retirement. Indeed, retirement may be a kind of liberation: emancipated from routine busyness, the retired person may be free for the first time to work and study passionately. The bleakness and emptiness that many of us, especially successful men, face upon retirement is a sad sign of spiritual impoverishment. The true self has been hidden and neglected for so long that it is withered and scarcely alive.

If we live long enough, the circle grows smaller too as friends and family die. I used to visit Nellie, who was nearing one hundred and who had come from Central Europe as a teenager. She had worked as a domestic, then married and raised two children who—in their professional achievements—epitomized the American dream. Now they too were elderly and of little practical or emotional support to Nellie. She could no longer walk well, but was in otherwise good health. Her mind was clear, and she was an excellent storyteller. I came to regard my visits to her as a kind of respite in a day of pastoring, a treat I promised myself after dutiful calls on other, less coherent residents. Her hair was always combed into a neat little bun, her posture was *very* upright, and her eyes twinkled behind round, steel-rimmed spectacles.

Nellie never complained. She had lived through so much pain and hardship that, like Paul, she was "content with weaknesses, insults, hardships, persecutions, and calamities" (2 Corinthians 12:10). One day, though, as her birthday approached and as staff members cheerily reminded her every day of the party they were planning, I found her depressed. She apologized, "I'm not good company today. You don't want to hear this." I assured her that I did and sat down to listen. "I shouldn't be complaining. They're good to me here. I have my own room, and the ladies from my church come to visit. I don't hurt much anywhere, either, just a little ache or two. I really shouldn't be complaining, but...." She paused. "Everybody's dead. All my friends are gone. Nobody remembers the same things I remember, and nobody really knows *me*. They just know a real old lady who doesn't have sense to get on with it and die."

There was really nothing to say. Nellie would not appreciate platitudes. We sat together in silence for a few moments, and she permitted a tear or two to appear behind the steel-rimmed spectacles. Then she patted my hand and said, "So the old friends are gone. There's not much I can do about that. But it's good to get new friends."

We can anticipate many losses when we are carried where we do not wish to go. There is loss of privacy, when a room must be shared with a stranger and when even the most gentle and attentive caregiver seems intrusive. There is the loss of possessions—neither Klara's books nor Pauline's used styrofoam cups were given up easily. The necessity of parting from a beloved pet, however unprepossessing and dilapidated in the eyes of others, is a poignant prefiguring of one's own mortality. There is the loss of home. When I visited new residents, this was often the most distressing part of their transition. It did not matter that home had been a shabby and neglected apartment in an increasingly dangerous neighborhood. It did not matter that their new surroundings were clean and bright, that good meals were served in an almost elegant dining room. They grieved for home—broken pipes, cockroaches, and falling plaster notwithstanding.

Most basic of all and to some extent the sum of all the concomitant losses is the loss of a carefully crafted identity. For women of an earlier generation, this may be related to marital status—I learned early to be very careful not to address a proud and independent spinster as "Mrs." and to be equally careful not to deny widows the same honorific. For others, identity is closely tied up with occupation: when they are no longer professionally active, when they are no longer perceived by themselves and by society as "useful," their identity is lost. There is great pain and diminishment in being known only as an "old person" or a "stroke victim" or a "shut-in." My friend Ellen was a dancer and, in my eyes, remained a dancer until her death, but in the eyes of the world and particularly of her parish, she was very much a "shut-in."

A friend who is a chaplain in a large nursing home for the very frail aged gave me a powerful image when he described his method for training theological students. "I tell them to visit with the residents, talk to them, and hear their stories. And when they ask me what to do about those who are unable to speak, unable to hear, perhaps even unconscious, I tell them the same thing: sit with them and listen to their stories. Each of those very old people, no matter how fragile their hold on life might be and no matter how *useless* they might be in the eyes of society, is a rare parchment. A rare parchment waiting to be read."

The Fruits of Loss

When I was a child, one of my staple items of reading was Eleanor Porter's *Pollyanna*, the story of an orphan who suffered all manner of adversity but managed at each distressing turn to find something to be "glad" about. Eventually she won the hearts of all around her, including her dour caretaker-aunt, and effected their conversion—not to Christianity, but to the "gospel of gladness." It is a cloying book, and Pollyanna's name has entered the language to signify a glib and mindless optimist.

It is tempting to be glib, especially when the misfortune is not ours. Indeed, we may think it our "Christian duty" to deny affliction and to rush toward joy, forgetting that a dark and somber thread runs through joy. Forgetting, in other words, that joy in Christ bears little resemblance to Pollyanna's gladness. I am convinced that "It's all for the best" and "Look on the bright side" should be stricken from the vocabulary of official and unofficial pastors, as well as from our own inner conversations when we feel compelled to deny the pain of loss. Desolation cannot be hurried; faith can survive it. Uncomfortable as it is, there is a time when we must let loss be loss, when we must "sit still, even among these rocks," in the words of T. S. Eliot's "Ash Wednesday."

There is no short cut out of the desert. The rocks there are real. So I want to tread very cautiously when I speak of the fruits of loss. What can be good about your life caving in? What can be good about living with diminished mobility and ever fewer choices, the loss of autonomy and the increase of dependence? Most poignant in the life of the frail aged and the very ill is their loss of control over even minor aspects of their own lives: what and when they will eat, whether they see the outdoors or even go outside their own rooms, when they will lie down and when they will sit up.

Yet one of the great and most obvious fruits of loss is simplification. As the extraneous falls away, priorities change; the essential, what really matters, stands out in sharp relief. For me this has been one of the joys of ministering with people at life's threshold. The very old and the very sick who are able to embrace loss and live through desolation are often willing, even eager to deal with the issues of deep meaning. In contrast to those of us whose lives are still crowded with activity, they are no longer distracted by the stimuli that swarm around us. In consequence, they become clear and candid. We may, of course, resist their clarity and candor if it threatens us. If our unease in the face of their directness leads us to such a choice, we have deprived ourselves of invaluable teachers. We may continue as conscientious visitors, bringing cheer and casual chat, but we have missed the opportunity to learn from the rich parchments before us, waiting to be read.

The Return to Holy Ground

Every now and then, at unexpected moments, the certain knowledge of my death pierces me. I look at my grandchildren and realize that some day they will be grown, middle-aged, and then old—and that I will have become a story they might tell to their children and grandchildren. I look at my accumulation of books and know that I will not have time to read all the favorites again. The practical, sensible me knows that it is time to start giving them away; but thus far my attempts to do this have been half-hearted. Sometimes I wake at dawn, that threshold time when God is very near but fear and emptiness are also hovering, and I know, deep within myself, that I am mortal.

John Keats, not yet twenty-five and dying of tuberculosis, began a sonnet, "When I have fears that I may cease to be...." The beginning of his poem is better than its end; despite his creative genius, he was unable to complete the sentence in a convincing and satisfying way. I suspect that it cannot be completed, that we must wait and grope and hope.

It is not easy to look into the abyss. Most of the time I would rather not, even when I know that the mysterious tug of God is pulling me toward that empty place. It is tempting to procrastinate, easy to vow—implicitly if not explicitly—"I will attend to the holy later, when the distractions are not so absorbing; I will let myself be undefended and open to the Infinite and Unknowable when I feel just a little wiser or stronger or more devout." We can be encouraged by the example of friends who have let us walk a little of the way with them, strengthened by the promise of Scripture and guided by the words of the mystics. But ultimately the journey toward a good death is a solitary journey, not without its terrors.

About six hundred years earlier, the Dominican Meister Eckhart preached a sermon based on Luke's account of the boy Jesus in the temple, when the twelve-year-old had stayed behind, to the consternation of his parents. Eckhart uses this familiar story to expand upon one of his favorite themes: the birth of God in the soul, in the empty place of abandonment and solitude. So he cautions his hearers, who may have been Dominican nuns under his spiritual direction:

> If you want to experience this birth, the encounter with God in your soul, you must leave the "crowd," that is, the company of kinsfolk and acquaintances traveling home from Jerusalem. And you must return to the origin and the ground from which you have come.[3]

Eckhart goes on to explain that the "crowd" is all those distractions, by no means evil or destructive in and of themselves, which keep us from this last step toward God. The crowd, according to Eckhart, is memory, reason, the senses, imagination, "everything in which you find yourself."

---

3 Josef Quint, trans. and ed., *Meister Eckehart: Deutsche Predigten und Traktate* (Munich: Diogenes, 1979), p. 433. Translation mine.

If Eckhart is right, we must leave that attractive and absorbing crowd. And we must return to the ground from which we came. "Ground"—*grund*—is one of his favorite words. It suggests many things: depth, darkness, and the solidity of the bed stone. It is our place of origin. It is holy ground. This is the place to which, when the extraneous has been let go, we return.

Whether it be journey, quest, or pilgrimage, we are embarked on a voyage of exploration. Explorers move into unknown territory. They may have heard stories and seen old maps, but they do not really know what they will find. Explorers are people of faith—they believe in the unseen and the uncharted. In the eyes of the world, they are often a little crazy and rarely practical. Some are greedy, lured by stories of hidden treasure. The explorer in Christ is greedy too, hungering above all else for God and willing to travel over strange terrain to return to the origin and ground from which she has come.

Like the prodigal son, we "come to ourselves," and like him, we yearn to go home. In German obituaries, "going home" is an expression comparable to our "passing away." But unlike the American euphemism, with its careful avoidance of the realities of life and death, "going home" is what it is all about. And quite possibly we are not fully grown up until just before our arrival, when we finally return to our origin and the holy ground from which we came.

Chapter Six

Ministry with the Aged

A s is clear throughout this book, I have been privileged to work among the very old and have been enriched by their friendship. They have been my teachers and my textbooks, letting me travel with them and join them in imagination when they reach a place not yet accessible to me. In fact, my ministry with them has really been an exchange of gifts: I have brought them my attentiveness and my respect, and they have given me a glimpse, indeed the vicarious experience of life at the second threshold. Much of what the frail aged have taught me can be translated to other situations: there are significant differences, to be sure, but also remarkable similarities in any ministry with those suffering from terminal or even serious chronic illness, regardless of age.

In the title of this chapter, which is a brief summary of some practical learnings, I have been deliberate in my choice of a preposition: I am writing about ministry *with*, not *to*, the aged. Good ministry, like spiritual friendship, is mutual; it is a dance, a drama, a story, a partnership. Ministry with the very old is enriching because of its immediacy. With the narrowing of the circle comes simplification. In the most active stages of our lives, we live in a forest of stimuli—absorbing, demanding, delightful, disturbing, and very often distracting. Colleagues in parish ministry and especially those working with youth tell me of the ongoing competition for attention and commitment; there are so many claims on time and energy, so many avenues to pursue that the call from God can be denied or drowned out. For the very old, however, seeming (and very real) loss can result in a willingness, even eagerness, to deal with the areas of deep concern. I have found that once even a modicum of trust has been established, the pastoral relationship is candid and direct.

Mortality is a profoundly theological issue. Perhaps it is *the* theological issue—at least from our limited human perspective. Certainly, making sense of one's life is a theological project and by no means the exclusive property of churchgoers. So it is not surprising that conversation with the aged, if it progresses beyond polite banalities, moves almost easily to the essentials: Has my life mattered? Am I known to God? For that matter, *is* there a God? What will it be like to die?

For the very old and sick, death is no longer the enemy. Again and again I have heard, "I've lived long enough...I'm tired...I'm ready...I'm not afraid of death—I'm afraid of pain or helplessness or incontinence or losing my mental powers." Death may not be the enemy, but dying can be frightening and hard. One of the greatest gifts we can bring to the aged is our willingness simply to listen when they talk about the approach of death. Because of our own discomfort, it is tempting to deny reality and urge a falsely cheery optimism.

I did not know Mrs. Stone until I met her in a hospital ward in her mid-eighties. She was lucid, but physically frail; she had been hospitalized for observation, since her physician could find no specific illness. When I stopped by her bed, she said, "I'm dying, and no one will believe me. My doctor says I'll be out of here in no time, and the nurses just try to jolly me along and ask, 'So what does it feel like?' Then they haven't time to listen when I try to tell them." She had told me herself what I needed to say; I sat down and asked, "So what *does* it feel like?" She pondered a bit, then said, "I can't quite explain it, but I just feel different. I know that something is going to happen, is happening. I don't want anything, I just want someone to take me seriously." We talked for a while. I agreed to speak to her sister, her only relative and living in a distant city, and to stop by the next time I was on duty. When I came back in a few days, Mrs. Stone had died.

The aged may make us uncomfortable because we are not ready to enter their stripped and simplified spiritual environment. We are not ready for the starkness of living on the edge. This strikes me especially at holiday times when garish decorations are put up weeks ahead of the festive day. Mrs. Koch, a tough old lady with the face of a saint and a distinctly unsaintly vocabulary, made it clear to me that such attempts at cheer benefited the staff more than the aged residents when she observed, "Honey, I can't wait till they take these goddam decorations down. They depress the hell out of me. What can be merry about Christmas when you can hardly move and you hurt all over all the time?"

As pastors or companions to the aged (or to anybody living on the threshold) we must face ourselves and know ourselves. We must face the fact of our own mortality and befriend it if we are to minister to those who are facing death. Only then can our ministry be honest, based on the stark solidity of bed stone. Not everyone is comfortable with "God-talk," nor does everyone have the vocabulary. But we should be able to hear the questions of life and death, the "God-questions," even when the specialized vocabulary is not present. We can sort out true prayer—Help! Where are you? Why have you forsaken me? God, you bastard!—from pious repetitions. We can listen to what is not said and be aware of the great empty places. Perhaps we will never speak of our insight or raise direct questions, but we need to notice what is being avoided as the story is told. We can give gentle permission for candor and create a safe space.

Listening to the Stories

Stories have been important in my ministry with the aged, and my role has almost always been that of listener—passive, receptive, and attentive. I realize now that my training started early: my maternal grandmother was a natural storyteller, with a vivid sense of scene and amazing recall (or creation?) of detail. My parents, especially my mother, had heard all the stories many times and must have groaned inwardly when Grandma launched into an account of how her Great-Uncle Flavius (whom she knew only from *her* grandmother's stories) had died at an early age of a mysterious fever. Poor Flavius—so young, so handsome, so talented; and he never had a chance! (Decades later family piety led me to seek out his grave in a little Vermont cemetery.)

I heard stories of pioneer days in Illinois, Uncle Sam Ritchie's adventures in the California gold rush—his trick knee went out while he was crossing the desert—and the day Grandma's brother Henry, the mischievous one, took a bag of flying squirrels to the one-room school. Her stories reached back many years before her own birth, helped her make sense of a lifetime of experience stretching from the Civil War to the outbreak of World War II, and knit her own story into *the* story of family. I couldn't hear them often enough. Far from being boring, repetition became a kind of liturgical reinforcement, deepening and enriching the simple narratives.

The spirituality of the aged is a spirituality of storytelling. Telling the story brings the past, present, and future together. Telling the story breathes life into a time of closure and seeming diminishment. Long after my grandmother's death, I again found myself sitting quietly and listening to stories of times and people long gone. There were tragic tales of loss and pain, but also joyous bits of memory, clear and immediate.

Oscar, a very old Scandinavian, was watching the snow swirl past the nursing home window and fall to the grimy street ten floors below. He never talked much, but that day he felt like visiting. "You know," he said, "we lived on a farm. We were poor, but my daddy made us a sled. And there was snow in the winter those days, there was snow! And we'd take that sled out on the hill—there was only one hill, but it was pretty good, and what a time we'd have! I can still remember how it felt, going down that hill." I didn't need to say anything, and I knew that too much enthusiasm could seem patronizing to this dignified and normally taciturn old man. So we just sat and watched the snow for a while.

I loved those times of listening. I was invited into sacred space, invited for a little while to *be* there in the story. Sometimes it was sad, sometimes poignant, and sometimes delightful. Mary had been an art teacher, but now she was confined to a wheelchair and was quite disoriented. Or at least, the staff regarded her as disoriented because she was not sure where she was or who was currently President. But when I stopped to sit with her for a bit, we were both whisked back to Paris in the 1920s. "I met Isadora Duncan, and I took off my shoes and danced for her. She said I had promise." Isadora Duncan paled, however, beside Mary's gentleman friend, an exiled Russian prince named Vladimir. I am not sure whether the flesh-and-blood Vladimir could have been so suave and charming as the prince of her memories, but Mary's stories were better than anything blaring on the television in the dayroom. As I stood to leave, she looked around her half of the little room—the side without the window—and said, "You know, my dear, this is the nicest cruise I've been on. I'm glad you're aboard." I was glad that I was aboard, too.

The spirituality of the aged is a spirituality of completion. We are never finished products, and many of the very old are still struggling with relationships, even or especially with people long dead, as they work toward wholeness and closure.

So I have encountered adult children of alcoholics well into their nineties and still children despite their frail, deteriorating bodies. I have met aged orphans who still mourn their state. One day Nellie, my hundred-year-old friend from Czechoslovakia, was reminiscing about the death of her mother. As she told the story, the years melted away; I could almost see the frightened and baffled six-year-old watching the coffin being carried through the front door of the house, the door never used except to admit a bride or a dead body. This strong woman, who had worked and sacrificed without complaint, had never forgotten the pain of abandonment. She was still working on what it meant to be an orphan.

Patience and Timing

Not all the stories reached so far into the past. Some of my friends mourned the loss of a much-loved home, the death of an adult child, or—most poignantly—the death of the person who had shared their daily lives. We tend to be impatient with grief so that the loss of a spouse or lifetime companion is dismissed quickly—except by the bereaved. Here as pastors we can bring the gift of time and patience, listening to the stories and acknowledging by our compassionate presence that there are no quick fixes or easy answers.

Such a gift cannot be underestimated. Even the kindest caregivers are usually in a great and unavoidable hurry. The bedside attendants in nursing homes and hospitals carry a heavy burden if they are to give adequate *physical* care to those in their charge. However well-intentioned they might be, there is practically never time to sit down and listen. Family members, too, are likely to be overloaded with responsibility and stress. They may be struggling with resentment and its concomitant guilt; spending time listening to the story—already overfamiliar—may be impossible for them.

Even if we are in a hurry too, we can create a sense of spaciousness and abundant time. This may simply be a matter of posture—do we sit down or do we hover? It is important to re-member the helplessness of a person lying in bed or sitting immobile in a wheelchair. The presence of an active, vigorous person, standing firmly on two feet and looming above, can be overwhelming. So it is always good to sit, if only briefly, and having first asked permission. When we visit, we are ex-tending hospitality by our gift of attentive presence, but at the same time, we are guests.

Among the almost inevitable losses of frail old age are pri-vacy and autonomy. This may mean sharing a small room with a stranger; it may mean the constant presence of a caregiver; it almost certainly means that all sorts and condi-tions of people—physicians, nurses, technicians, nurses' aides, cleaners, and kitchen help delivering trays—will enter the room without knocking. The last bit of private space is the few square feet around the bed or wheelchair, and even that is rarely private. The frail aged are necessarily touched, usu-ally impersonally, not always gently and rarely lovingly, by those in charge of their intimate care. We need to remember that we are entering another's private space and should not assume that we have been invited.

So we ask: "Is this a good time?" It usually is, but it is im-portant to be attentive to meal and rest times. It is distinctly uncomfortable for an old person, perhaps already impaired by a stroke or arthritis, to struggle with utensils and to try to carry on a conversation while a relative stranger is watching. Deal-ing with a tray of food is hard work for the frail aged and is best done without distraction, unless of course the visitor can be tactfully helpful. When you are comfortable together, offers of assistance might be gratefully accepted: the visitor can move the tray to a more accessible position, perhaps butter the bread and cut the meat, and pour out the coffee or tea. Not to the rim—two-thirds full is easiest to handle.

No matter how tight the schedule might be, we can avoid communicating haste. We can create a sense of spaciousness

by how we breathe or speak. At the same time, we can cultivate the art of patient listening. I have found that old people
usually speak slowly. Even when their minds are keen, the
words do not come quickly; and the speech of a person who
has suffered a stroke may be especially labored. So we need
to be willing to wait and to be comfortable in long pauses. It is
tempting to assume that we understand, even to hurry to
complete the other's sentence.

George, a former professor and author of several books,
suffered from his caregiver's impatience. Alone with a close
friend and old colleague, he managed to say—slowly, of
course: "These young people don't take time to listen. They
think I'm just another senile old man. We all look alike, I
guess, once we're here. I can't get a sentence out, certainly
can't finish one, once I've started. Then I get rattled. It's just
not worth the trouble."

Tucked into Mark's account of Jesus healing the blind beggar Bartimaeus are two unremarkable little words. I had
skipped over them for years until a friend, who works with the
mentally retarded, pointed them out. When the blind man
called out, "Jesus, son of David, have mercy on me," *Jesus
stopped.* He didn't say, "Walk along beside me, and we'll talk
as we go." He didn't say, "We'll talk when we get to Jericho."
He didn't deputize a disciple to assess the situation. He
stopped, and he listened. Mark doesn't tell us how long the
pause lasted; indeed, its length is not important. But for just a
few moments, perhaps only for a moment, the blind man had
Jesus' total attention. For just a few moments, time stood still,
and there was all the time in the world.

When we are with the aged, we try to be caring but disinterested listeners. Just to listen is enough. We are not there to
talk them out of their anger, disappointment, and fears.
Rather, we need to be open to everything they might say and
to take everything seriously. Too often we are guilty of treating
the aged as we treat children: we do not listen, or we listen

distractedly, and then we patronize in our responses. Neither the very old nor the very young deserve such condescension.

I find in myself a "polite" inclination to want to make everything better, perhaps as cheap comfort to the other and most certainly as comfort to myself. This can lead me to minimize the other person's experience, forgetting that any burden carried over the years or any absorbing concern in the present *matters.* I cannot use my own experience as a yardstick since the frail aged are in a place I know only in imagination and anticipation. Guilt over a seemingly trivial offense or wounded feelings nursed for years, perhaps decades, are not to be glossed over and lightly dismissed. "That was a long time ago" or "Why don't you just forget about it?" are neither helpful nor compassionate responses. If we are unable to take the story seriously, we do not bring comfort, but diminishment.

When we value aged persons and let ourselves be open to them, our conversations can be a prayerful activity even when no prayers are spoken. Sometimes I do my praying before the visit begins, while coming up the stairs or before knocking on the door: "Let me be present and attentive...Let me put myself out of the way...Let me find Christ in this person...Let me mirror Christ for him." Occasionally, the prayer of preparation borders on the desperate. Before visiting Irma, who was querulous and chronically depressed, I would find myself praying: "Just let me get through this! Let me do no harm!" Irma had every right to be depressed: she had lived for and through her husband, and now he had died. In the early stages of her grief, stretching now into the second year, she saw no purpose in living. Her depression was contagious, and she had become increasingly isolated as friends dropped away one by one. It helped me a bit simply to understand what was happening: that Irma was caught in her own grief, that she had not been a cheerful person even in her best days, and that she *might* some day move to a moderately happy frame of mind, given time and patience.

I have also encountered people who are angry with the church, who feel neglected or ill-used by the religious establishment. Alec was a crotchety old man, nominally an Episcopalian but long alienated from his parish. When I first entered his hospital room, he growled, "What are you selling?" Before I could reply, he added, "And don't try to convert me—I'm not buying!" I promised him I wouldn't bother him and that I had only stopped to say "Hello." I decided that Alec didn't want the services of a chaplain and that God knew where he was, so I didn't call again until one of the nurses said, "I think he *really* wants to see you." After that, I visited him regularly during his long hospitalization. He still growled, but it was a friendly growl: "Hi, Toots. What are you peddling today?" God was never mentioned, and we certainly never prayed together in any recognized sense; but Alec talked about his pain and fear and eventually about his approaching death. I never learned why he was so angry at the church; it no longer seemed to matter. I learned quickly that he had no patience with sentimentality and that he didn't like to be fussed over. He needed to complain—"bitch" was his term—without being subjected to explanations or interpretations of why his life was ending the way it was. He was a tough old man, and we became good friends. I wonder how he is faring in heaven; I hope none of his fellow saints ever tries to hug him!

Some Practical Points for Pastoral Visitors

As I noted at the beginning of this chapter in the story of Mrs. Stone, many caregivers and family members are reluctant to talk about death or to listen while the dying person articulates her experience. We need to be attentive to indirect references and then not to shrink from saying the word "death." Once the barriers are down and the forbidden "D-word" has been uttered, the conversation becomes surprisingly easy. The very old person may exhibit curiosity: "What will it be like?" To which the pastoral visitor's honest answer must be, "I don't know, but I wonder too." Planning a funeral service together need not be a lugubrious task. Indeed, it can be an occasion for storytelling and companionship as favorite hymns and Scripture passages are selected.

I have learned to take my clues from my aged friends regarding spoken prayer. Some expect it, while others are embarrassed and uncomfortable at the prospect. For many, there is great comfort in familiar, well-worn prayers. The very old know much of the older prayer book by heart, so I encourage my young colleagues to equip themselves with a copy and become at home in it. Similarly, for the very old the King James Version is *the* Bible, regardless of the claim to accuracy of the later translations.

A large-print Bible, prayer book, or hymnal can be a welcome gift. The American Bible Society is a valuable source of inexpensive Bibles in various translations and type sizes. The King James Version is available on audiocassette, a boon for the visually impaired, provided that the cassette player is easy to manipulate and can be kept close at hand. This is not to be taken for granted: when I suggested that one of the nursing home's blind residents would enjoy listening to my set of the tapes, my offer was refused: "A tape player, even a cheap one, wouldn't last a day in her room. And we'd never be able to find out who took it." Miss Emery's few square feet of private space were sadly insecure.

Faithful ministry with the aged is bound to stir up feelings in the visitor. I have already noted the contagious nature of depression. If I find myself bored, unusually tired, and resistant at the prospect of visiting someone, I can be fairly sure that I am absorbing some of that person's depression. I have to fight my tendency toward impatience and remind myself, again and again, that grief cannot be hurried and that the old person may be justifiably saddened by tremendous loss. It is an act of simple charity for me to acknowledge the enormity of that loss; such an acknowledgment might even lift the burden a bit. It is important to remember too that a number of common medications have depression as a side-effect and that the very old are especially susceptible.

In my relationships with aged friends I frequently experience feelings of guilt: I do not visit often enough. Or stay long enough. Or have anything to offer a life that seems bleak and empty. And how guilty I feel when I walk away briskly, perhaps pausing at the elevator door to wave good-bye to the person watching from a wheelchair! Not only do I feel guilty, I feel cheap! I have given a few minutes, even an hour of my time—and then I get on with a busy life. When I pick apart my feelings of guilt, I know that I am frightened: What will my life be like if, when I am immobile? How will I feel about cheerful people who pop into my day and then disappear, expecting me to be grateful for their fleeting attention? I have no easy solutions for such pangs of guilt, except to name them and live with them, and to try to be faithful in my commitment to my friends.

I have learned the hard way to be careful with specific promises. Tempting as it is to offer assurance of a speedy return, it is dangerous to say, "I will be back to see you at 3 o'clock next Tuesday." Next Tuesday might find me with a messy (and communicable) cold or unexpected work pressures or an unanticipated family crisis. Then I have promised more than I can deliver and have raised expectations irresponsibly, even cruelly. It is much better to say, "I always like visiting with you. I'll be back as soon as I can. I'll try for next week, but I really can't promise." If the visit is delayed, a card or a note keeps the conversation alive.

Touch is a sensitive issue. Desmond Morris, the animal behaviorist, has written persuasively about the irresistible charm of small mammals—puppies, kittens, and human babies: we *want* instinctively to touch and hold them. The aged are not irresistibly cute, yet they also need and yearn for a loving human touch. There are gradations of intimacy, of course: we can hold a hand while talking or praying together. (Gently, though. That old hand may be racked with arthritis.) A hug or a kiss on the cheek at meeting or parting may be welcome. But when I worked in the nursing home, I learned to be careful: by no means did everyone welcome the touch of a relative stranger. Peggy, the extrovert who greeted all visitors enthusiastically, would throw her arms around me—and everybody else—with surprising strength. Sometimes her exuberant embrace left me breathless, and I would try gently to peel her off. On the other hand, her dignified neighbor down the hall, Miss Nelson, was disgusted by what she perceived as tasteless displays of shallow affection. I realized quickly that she was delighted with a formal handshake. Once she was sure that I wasn't going to hug her, we got on splendidly.

Miss Nelson and Peggy illustrate another sensitive area: terms of address. Peggy liked the coziness of Christian names. She didn't like being called "Honey" or "Dear" by people who had no real affection for her, but she was happy to be called by the name her family and friends had used for seventy-five years. So when we met, she was always "Peggy" and I was always "Margaret." I am comfortable using Christian names, even of people much older than I, so long as the arrangement is mutual. It makes me uneasy, however, to hide behind a title or honorific; my work ceases to be ministry *with* and becomes ministry *to* my aged friends. So it was important to me that our use of first names be mutual.

Miss Nelson, on the other hand, would have been affronted by my casual use of her Christian name, just as she would have been distressed if I had carelessly called her "Mrs." or—horrors!—"Ms." Her body and her name were her last bastions of private space. At the very least, I could honor them. So she remained "Miss Nelson" and I was "Chaplain Guenther." Miss Nelson was a quintessential WASP, but in her insistence on correct use of titles she resembled many older African Americans who are affronted by inappropriate use of their Christian names. The pastoral visitor needs to remember that this is the residue of centuries of indignity, when adult men and women were diminished by condescending and over-familiar forms of address. What seems like easy friendliness in the white community can be insulting to people of color, especially when the racial lines are crossed.

Forty percent of people over seventy-five have some degree of hearing impairment, with men affected more frequently than women. I had always found it stressful to talk with the hearing impaired. Was I too loud? Too soft? Was I treating my conversation partner as if he were mentally deficient as well as deaf? And why did it take so much energy? Was it as hard on him as it was on me? Mr. Miller, who managed to remain highly gregarious despite his deafness, was the unofficial consciousness-raiser for the hearing visitor to the nursing home. He became my good-natured teacher, reminding me of things I should have known instinctively. "Look directly at the other person while you speak. Don't cover your mouth with your hand. And for heaven's sake, don't mumble! And don't get impatient if you are asked to repeat what you have already said twice. And remember, deaf people like to visit. We get lonesome too, you know."

I make a point of noticing the environment when I enter the room, whether in a nursing home or a private house. It tells me a lot about the quality of the aged person's life and the care she is receiving. Is there a tray of dirty dishes left long after meal time? Are there flowers and plants, and are they fresh and healthy? (A moribund plant or wilted cut flowers can erode the most cheerful temperament.) Is there a radio or television? These can be welcome links with the active world and a source of pleasure and mental stimulation. They can also be an unwelcome source of noise and confusion, especially if they are left on by caregivers to fill the silence. I remember the irony of a group of very frail and confused old women lined up before the dayroom television set blaring a rerun of "The Dating Game." And there was the time I was summoned to say the commendatory prayers for a woman who had died in her late eighties. As I signed her with the cross and prayed, "Depart, O Christian soul out of this world," the eminent pediatrician and author Berry Brazelton loudly held forth on baby care from the television mounted opposite her bed. I wondered, "Had she chosen the program? Did she even know that it was on?" Probably not.

I always look for signs of family involvement and affection. Are cards and children's artwork displayed? And are they recent, or yellowed with age? Family pictures tell a great deal and provide an opening for conversation. "Tell me about..." is usually enough to get the story going, and it's always a good idea to admire babies lavishly.

We all like to receive gifts, especially unexpected ones. For the homebound and those living in institutions, simple gifts are a tangible statement of care and connection. Flowers and plants bring a bit of outdoors and a sense of the changing seasons. Much as I love the heady fragrance of hyacinths and other spring flowers, though, I have learned to be careful. For some, the fragrance is delightful, almost as good as a visit to a bygone garden; but for others, it can be overwhelming in an enclosed room.

Newsletters and taped sermons help maintain a relationship with the parish. We need to be sure that the recipient can read the fine print of the newsletter, however, and has the necessary equipment to listen to the tape. When her pastoral visitor asked one homebound woman how he could be helpful, she replied, "You can begin by reading me this pile of stuff I have from the parish. I'd love to know what's happening, but I can't make it out."

Books, especially large print, are good, but it important for the giver to know tastes and interests. The amateur oenologist is unlikely to be interested in backstairs accounts of the House of Windsor, and the mystery fan may spurn the historical romance. Stamps and writing materials are also welcome. More meaningful and more generous than gifts of books and writing paper, however, is the offer of our own time: to read to the visually impaired and to write letters for those no longer able to manage a pen can be more welcome than any tangible gift.

One of the best gifts we can give is to enable the frail aged person to be a giver. Rae, one of my nursing home friends, proudly gave me a chocolate bar from time to time. At first I resisted: her spending money was very limited, and I was not sure that I should accept anything from her. Further, a chocolate bar was the last thing in the world that I needed! But gradually I realized two things: Rae loved chocolate, so she was giving me the very best, the most delightful thing she could manage. And more important, Rae, who was crippled and confined to her wheelchair, became a whole woman again when she was able to give something away. Thereafter, I took the chocolate gratefully.

In the chapter on kinship, I have already written about commissioning the frail aged as intercessors. No more needs to be said here, except to note again that their prayers are perhaps the greatest gift they can give us.

Routine care of those who are bedfast or wheelchair-bound is difficult, often thankless work. Family members sacrifice time and spontaneity, while professional caregivers rank among the most poorly paid and least prestigious workers in our society. The cycle of work is endless: getting up, dressing, feeding, bathing, toileting, and preparing for bed. There is little time and usually even less psychic energy for leisurely conversation with the patient. The best efforts go unnoticed or are taken for granted, and thanks are rarely forthcoming. I still remember my barely suppressed rage when a well-meaning neighbor suggested that I spend more time with my invalid mother-in-law, who lived with us. At the time, I had a job, a house, a husband, and three young children, and I thought I was doing pretty well. Maybe not so well, but it was the best I could manage. A kind word rather than a critical one from my neighbor would have made a big difference.

Pastoral visitors can befriend and appreciate the caregivers as well. Merely learning an aide's name and inquiring after her well-being goes a long way toward establishing a warm relationship. Sometimes it feels right to include caregivers in prayers and celebrations of the eucharist, but sometimes the patient prefers to be alone with the visitor. Here again, I take my cue from the aged person.

Parishes need to make vigorous efforts to remember and include the homebound and institutionalized in the life of the parish. It is ironic how newcomers are consciously and enthusiastically cultivated: they are noticed, feted with parties and after-service brunches, visited, and befriended. Almost every parish has a committee whose sole work is to identify and keep track of them. By contrast, the frail aged disappear quietly: they come to services less frequently and then not at all. To be sure, they may be visited monthly by clergy or eucharistic ministers, but they are—as one of my activist friends puts it—shut-*outs,* not shut-*ins.*

I know of parishes that do work consciously to include the frail aged. They arrange Sunday transportation, increasingly a problem for even the relatively active as our society becomes ever more dependent on the private automobile. In addition to the customary pastoral visits at Christmas and Easter, they remember the homebound on special anniversaries—birthdays and, more important, the death dates of loved ones. They may offer help with living wills and funeral plans. They coordinate telephone ministries, often using the elderly homebound as volunteers. Finally, they turn to the aged themselves as active ministers of intercession.

There are many possibilities for active pastoral ministry to and with the frail aged. They are costly in time and commitment, but not in dollars and cents. For the ministry to be alive and genuine, those ministering must be convinced of the value of each person. They must take time to learn the stories. How can you really care about someone who is merely a name on a list?

"Each of those very old people, no matter how fragile their hold on life might be and no matter how *useless* they might be in the eyes of society, is a rare parchment," my chaplain friend told me. The aged among us are rare parchments, waiting to be read by those of us who will take the time to listen. We are honored to sit in their presence. And these rare parchments may indeed show us how we ourselves, God willing, might grow up to be rare parchments, too.

Resources

Aelred of Rievaulx. *Spiritual Friendship*. Kalamazoo, Mich.: Cistercian Publications, 1974.

Affirmative Aging: A Creative Approach to Longer Life, ed. Joan E. Lukens for the Episcopal Society for Ministry on Aging. Harrisburg, Pa.: Morehouse, 1994.

Ashley, Kathleen and Pamela Sheingorn, eds. *Interpreting Cultural Symbols: Saint Anne in Late Medieval Society*. Athens, Ga. and London: The University of Georgia Press, 1990.

Bianchi, Eugene. *Aging as a Spiritual Journey*. New York: Crossroad, 1982.

Conn, Joann Wolski. *Spirituality and Personal Maturity*. New York and Mahwah, N. J.: Integration Books, 1989.

Delany, Sarah L. and A. Elizabeth. *Having Our Say*. New York: Dell, 1993.

Eliot, T. S. *Four Quartets*. New York: Harvest/HBJ, 1971.

Hillesum, Etty. *An Interrupted Life*, tr. Arno Pomerans. New York: Pantheon, 1983.

Kidder, Tracy. *Old Friends*. New York: Houghton Mifflin, 1993.

Luke, Helen M. *Old Age*. New York: Parabola Books, 1987.

Mitchell, Stephen, tr. and ed. *Tao te Ching: A New English Version*. New York: HarperCollins, 1992.

Moore, Thomas. *Care of the Soul: A Guide for Cultivating Depth and Sacredness in Everyday Life*. New York: HarperCollins, 1992.

Nuland, Sherwin B. *How We Die: Reflections on Life's Final Chapter.* New York: Vintage Books, 1993.

Ourselves, Growing Older: Women Aging with Knowledge and Power, ed. Paula Brown Doress and Diana Laskin Siegal. New York: Touchstone, 1987.

The Oxford Book of Aging: Reflections on the Journey of Life, ed. Thomas R. Cole and Mary G. Winkler. New York: Oxford University Press, 1994.

Sarton, May. *After the Stroke: A Journal.* New York: W. W. Norton & Co., 1988.

Scott-Maxwell, Florida. *The Measure of My Days.* New York: Penguin, 1979.

Shaw, Luci. *God in the Dark: Through Grief and Beyond.* Grand Rapids, Mich.: Zondervan, 1989.

———. *Polishing the Petoskey Stone: New and Selected Poems.* Wheaton, Ill.: Howard Shaw Publishers, 1990.

Shakespeare, William. *King Lear.* Any edition.

———. *The Tempest.* Any edition.

Spark, Muriel. *Memento Mori.* New York: Avon, 1990.

Taylor, Jeremy. *Holy Dying,* ed. P. G. Stanwood. Oxford: Clarendon Press, 1989.

Truitt, Anne. *Daybook: The Journal of an Artist.* New York: Viking-Penguin, 1984.

Vanstone, C. H. *The Stature of Waiting.* New York: Seabury, 1983.

And, of course, the stories of your parents, grandparents, and aged friends, and your own memories.